THE 500 YEARS of RESISTANCE COMIC BOOK

GORD HILL

THE 500 YEARS OF RESISTANCE COMIC BOOK

GORD HILL

ARSENAL PULP PRESS | Vancouver

THE 500 YEARS OF RESISTANCE COMIC BOOK
Copyright © 2010 by Gord Hill
Introduction © 2010 by Ward Churchill

Fifth printing: 2016

ARSENAL PULP PRESS
#202-211 East Georgia St.
Vancouver, BC
Canada V6A 1Z6
arsenalpulp.com

The publisher gratefully acknowledges the support of the Canada Council for the Arts and the British Columbia Arts Council for its publishing program, and the Government of Canada through the Book Publishing Industry Development Program and the Government of British Columbia through the Book Publishing Tax Credit Program for its publishing activities.

Printed and bound in Canada

Library and Archives Canada Cataloguing in Publication

Hill, Gord, 1968-
        The 500 years of resistance comic book / Gord Hill.

ISBN 978-1-55152-360-6

        1. Indians—Government relations—History—Comic books, strips, etc. 2. Government, Resistance to-America—History—Comic books, strips, etc. 3. America—Colonization—Comic books, strips, etc. I. Title. II. Title: Five hundred years of resistance comic book.

E59.G6H54 2010   970.004'9700222   C2010-900740-9

PREFACE

Yo weeksus! My name is Gord Hill. I currently live in the Downtown Eastside of Vancouver, British Columbia, Canada (occupied Coast Salish territory). From the Kwakwaka'wakw nation, with Tlingit and Scottish ancestry, my family lineage includes the Hunt and Scow families. I have lived on reserves and in cities, small towns, and isolated mountain camps, and have been involved in Indigenous and other social movements since 1988, participating in many protests, occupations, and blockades. I am an artist, writer, and carver. Above all, I consider myself a warrior—one who defends his people and territory.

In order to understand the world we live in today, it is vital to know our history. Unfortunately, the history we are taught through the educational system and corporate entertainment industry is false, particularly its depiction of European colonization as inevitable (or even justified) and Indigenous peoples as helpless victims (or even willing participants). The story of our ancestors' resistance is minimized, at best, or erased entirely. This strategy has been used to impose capitalist ideology on people, to pacify them, and to portray their struggle as doomed to failure.

Over 500 years ago, various European powers began the invasion, occupation, and colonization of the Americas, setting in motion a process of genocide and destruction that continues to this day. Indigenous nations suffered drastic reductions in population, as much as ninety percent in most cases, the result of European warfare and disease. When the Americas were being invaded and colonized, Europe was in the grip of great economic and social upheavals, suffering widespread poverty, resource depletion, disease, and war. The invasion of the Americas revived a dying Europe, infusing it with new agricultural goods and resources such as gold and silver, as well as relieving its excess population through settlements in the "New World."

Today, the global economic and cultural dominance of Europe and its settler colonies, such as Canada and the US, is the result of this history of colonialism. Another indisputable consequence is the fact that throughout the world, Native peoples suffer the highest rates of poverty, suicide, homelessness, violent death, drug and alcohol addiction, disease, imprisonment, and dislocation. This is true whether one looks at Indigenous peoples in Chile, Canada, or Australia.

Yet our history also shows that our ancestors fought and inflicted many defeats upon European colonial forces. In some regions of the Americas, it took hundreds of years before European control was established. Even today, colonial states face ongoing Indigenous resistance. This legacy of resistance can inspire our people to continue to defend their territories and communities against ongoing colonial aggression.

The purpose of *The 500 Years of Resistance Comic Book* is to raise the levels of historical understanding and warrior spirit among Indigenous peoples and others. When we know and understand this history of oppression, we will be better able to fight the system it has created. Without a fighting spirit, we will have no will to resist (or even survive).

The strength of the comic book is that it uses minimal text with graphic art to tell the story. This format is useful in reaching children, youth, and adults who have a hard time reading books or lengthy articles. We use many diverse methods of communication—including newsletters, books, videos, music, posters, stickers, paintings, banners, and T-shirts—because no single one will be successful by itself.

I am grateful to the good people at Arsenal Pulp Press for this opportunity to share my art and writing with a broader public. I would also like to thank Dave Cunningham and Allan Antliff for pursuing efforts to get the comic published, and Ward Churchill for his valuable introduction.

I dedicate this comic to all Indigenous peoples, to our ancestors, and the future generations.

Long Live the Warrior!
Gilakas'la
Gord Hill, Kwakwaka'wakw
February 2010

REFLECTIONS ON GORD HILL'S *500 YEARS* AND THE NATURE OF INDIGENOUS RESISTANCE

Ward Churchill

I may as well admit, first of all, that I received the invitation to write an introduction to Gord Hill's "comic book" with a considerable degree of skepticism. Knowing his work in other connections, however, it seemed the least I could do was agree to have a look rather than simply dismissing the idea out of hand. Perhaps the result serves as proof of the old adage about never being too old to learn, but I'm certainly glad I did so, because his *500 Years of Resistance* turned out to be a revelation. Before I was halfway through, I'd come to the realization that it would be a privilege—indeed, an honor—to introduce this remarkable piece of work, the sophistication and communicative effectiveness of which has transformed my appreciation for the graphic approach to history.

The question then became how to go about it. After all, it's not like I've had a lot of experience with the medium at hand. Nonetheless, after some reflecting on the matter, I concluded that the answer was obvious enough. I've always sought to heed the counsel of Muscogee elder Philip Deere never to try to be someone—or some*thing*—you're not, but instead to always strive to be the very best of who you are. What follows is expressed in the voice I've long since found to be my own, with no attempt made to blend my idiom with Gord's. His voice is his, mine is mine, as it should and ultimately must be if either of our voices is to be of value, even to ourselves.

In the end, it seems to me that our distinctly different stylistic approaches to conveying information tend to be mutually reinforcing, each in a certain sense completing the other to produce something more nearly resembling a whole, far stronger together than either could hope to be on its own, so much so that I've come to suspect that Gord foresaw precisely this result. A better illustration of the fundamental truth of Sitting Bull's famous nineteenth-century observation that it is "unnecessary for crows to be eagles" and vice versa, which also makes it possible for non-Indians to fully understand and act upon this truth, is difficult to imagine. Herein lies the key to genuine respect between people, and between peoples as well.

As is customary, I will proceed by telling a story—a couple of stories, actually—although the manner in which I recount them by no means adheres to the form in which such things are customarily done in traditional settings. The reasons for this go back to the nature of Philip's advice to me all those years ago, and, in any case, the setting in which they're being told is anything but traditional. That said, however, their purpose is the same: To clarify, sometimes in a seemingly oblique fashion, the broader matter(s) before us.

YELLOW THUNDER

Back in the early 1980s, I was a participant in Dakota AIM's (American Indian Movement) sustained occupation of Wincanyan Zi Tiospaye (the Yellow Thunder Community), an 880-acre parcel of land in the Black Hills, about a dozen miles outside of Rapid City, South Dakota. The occupation was seen at the time as a first step in physically reclaiming the Hills, or the He Sapa (or Paha Sapa), as they are known to the Lakota, which were seized in 1877 by the United States in direct violation of the 1868 Fort Laramie Treaty. The stakes involved were exceedingly high.

For the Lakota, the Yellow Thunder occupation—named in memory of Raymond Yellow Thunder, a "Pine Ridge Sioux" (Oglala Lakota) man whose grisly torture/murder for the amusement of local whites in Gordon, Nebraska, galvanized regional Indian resistance in 1972—reflected a collective will to free themselves from such dehumanization and the subjugation to which they'd been forcibly reduced by the US during the late-nineteenth century.

To this end, the Lakota's unabashedly expressed goal, as manifested through the actions of Dakota AIM, were to recover, in its entirety, the He Sapa, sacred heartland of their traditional territory, thereby enforcing their treaty rights as a sovereign co-equal of the US and restoring themselves to a genuinely self-determining status, resulting in a renewed sense of personal dignity and self-esteem invariably attendant to decolonization and national liberation.

By contrast, the US interest in the Black Hills was first and foremost an economic one. The Hills themselves encompassed what were and still are believed to be among the most mineral-rich area on earth. By 1980, the Homestake Mining Corporation alone was estimated to have extracted more than $14 billion (US) in gold from a single vein near the town of Deadwood. Rich deposits of uranium, molybdenum, and other strategic metals had also been discovered, and plans were afoot to exploit them. In addition, the Hills' stunning natural beauty had spawned a lucrative and rapidly-growing tourist industry.

There were and are significant military interests as well. One of the Strategic Air Command's major bases, Ellsworth, was situated just outside Rapid City. Dense-pack missile silos have also been so heavily concentrated in the region that it was a standing joke among AIM members that, when it regained control over the 1868 Treaty Territory, the Lakota Nation would automatically become the world's third ranking nuclear power (behind the US, which would've still ranked first, and the Soviet Union; Britain, France, China, and Israel would have lagged far behind, while India and Pakistan were not yet really in the game).

At another level, it was and remains imperative for the US to maintain the doctrinal pretense that it enjoys the "legal right" to unilaterally exempt itself from inconvenient provisions in still-binding treaties, assert jurisdiction over the other nations party to such treaties, make disposition of their lands and other resources, reshape their governments, and disperse their populations at its pleasure. Should any one of the 500-odd Indigenous nations within the continental United States manage to accomplish what the Lakota were attempting, the precedent could very well result in an unraveling of the whole intricate web of legal mythology woven by the judiciary to lend the structure of US internal colonialism a façade of legitimacy.

Materially, the implications are staggering. In its 1979 final report, the federal government's Indian Claims Commission conceded that after three decades of intensive effort it had been unable to identify *any* legal basis upon which the US could claim title to roughly a third of the area comprising the forty-eight coterminous states. In effect, the federal government admitted that many of America's Indigenous nations have never ceded, sold, or otherwise lawfully relinquished their lands and still hold legal title to them. The US occupation of these territories is therefore illegal in very much the same sense as Iraq's 1990–91 occupation of Kuwait or Israel's ongoing occupation of the West Bank.

At the very least, the Yellow Thunder initiative stood to put all of this in play, clouding title not only to vast chunks of the "American homeland," but to crucial sectors of the US "domestic economy" as well, seriously impairing the efficiency of elite planning. The reclamation of these lands would result not only in a substantive reconfiguration of the relations between the US and the Indigenous nations upon whose lands and with whose resources it has constructed and maintained itself, but within the North American settler polity itself and, as a consequence, between the US and the rest of the world.

The vision was undeniably expansive, and its actualization no doubt far beyond anything reasonably within the reach of the few dozen Natives bent upon pursuing it in the face of all odds, but that was how we saw it at the moment. This "moment" was sustained through four years of continuous occupation, through the frozen depths of multiple winters with little more than the canvas walls of tents and tipis to cut the force of South Dakota's eternally-driving winds and to defend us against the early sniping of local racists—looking back, it seems a wonder that only one of them, a camouflage-clad thug named Clarence Tollefson, was killed—and the constant threat of air assaults by federal SWAT units. The moment was further sustained in jail cells and through seemingly endless rounds of judicial proceedings.

Eventually, the occupation ended, not because the government was ever able to force us from the land—actually, by refusing to back down, we'd been able to wring an unprecedented decision by a federal district court that we had every right to remain there—but through a revealing sort of dissipation. As time wore on, key individuals were increasingly siphoned off to do the "international work" of seeking formal recognition of Lakota sovereignty from Third World governments and to facilitate codification of Indigenous rights international law through the United Nations. While neither of these efforts ultimately panned out, they ultimately overstretched Dakota AIM's capacity to retain focus and cohesion.

The problem was greatly amplified when, beginning in 1984, a dispute arose among North American Native dissidents of various denominations over whether the self-determining rights of Indigenous nations are actually inherent, or if they are something more "situational" or "contingent." In other words, do such rights prevail only when a usurping settler state embraces capitalism? Are they in some sense qualified or invalidated altogether by the fact that the usurping state purports to be socialist or communist?

Such questions were a result of a drive by Nicaragua's revolutionary Sandinista government to incorporate the country's Indigenous peoples into its unitary structure, thus subsuming those peoples' resistance. By and large, North America's settler Left responded by supporting the Sandinistas while vociferously denouncing the Indians as "contras" (a slur that even hardline Sandinista Interior Minister Tómas Borgé rejected as a gross over-simplification). In short order, we found ourselves confronted by people who'd previously claimed to be among our staunchest allies with the ab-surd—but nonetheless repeatedly articulated—proposition that "the success of the revolution is more important to securing Indian rights than the Indians themselves."

It was in some ways as if a switch had been thrown. One day we were receiving what seemed to be solid support, the next—since we remained unequivocal in asserting, as we always had, that Indigenous rights are un-changed by the ideological complexion of our colonizers—the opposite was true. The donations needed to fund the logistical requirements of a protracted occupation dried up almost immediately, while organizational commitments to underwriting portions of our legal offensive were mysteriously withdrawn. Where at first we'd been acclaimed for mounting one of the most concrete domestic challenges to US power, now we were suddenly branded as "CIA agents."

To describe the abruptness of the shift as disconcerting would be a radical understatement. The extent to which we'd misjudged the solidarity or reliability of our "friends" had a profoundly disquieting effect on many of us, compelling our mutual recognition of the need to step back, think through what had happened, identify and correct our more fundamental mistakes, and, as a result, devise new approaches to accomplishing what we'd set out to do. This represented neither failure nor defeat, but instead a stock-taking of lessons learned.

While it is an unfortunate reality that a few individuals identified with AIM seized upon the period of turmoil during the mid-'80s as an opportunity to cash in, demanding substantial fees to publicly align themselves with assorted leftist parties—some later resorting to the incorporation of their own "AIM" franchises in order to collect governmental/corporate subsidies—none of them played an active role in Yellow Thunder. As for those of us who did, it should by now be clear that we believed not only in what we were doing, but in the principles that led us to do it. And, without exception, so far as I know, we still do.

Nowhere is this more apparent than among the Lakota people, whose charge Dakota AIM accepted in undertaking the occupation. They have, among other things, engaged in the longest continuous legal battle to recover stolen land of any Native people. Stripped of some ninety percent of their treaty territory by the end of the nineteenth century, the Lakota filed the first briefs asserting their right to recover the He Sapa in 1923, and, generation after generation, with undeviating insistence, they've pursued that goal through the maze of US judicial obfuscation ever since.

In 1975, the Lakota were finally able to force the federal government's Indian Claims Commission to admit that the entire region had been illegally taken from them, at which point they were awarded what the government estimated to have been the cash value of the land at the time it was taken—$17.5 million for roughly 134 million acres—as "just compensation" for their loss. The US government appealed, but the Supreme Court upheld the decision. However, the Lakota emphatically came to the conclusion that "the Black Hills are not for sale." Apparently stunned by the refusal of a monetary settlement from a people generally considered to be one of the most impoverished on the continent, the Supreme Court took the matter "under advisement."

Five years later, having decided to up the ante dramatically, the high court weighed in with a "final offer" of $122.5 million, an amount computed by adding a century's worth of simple interest to the "already established" principle amount. When the Lakota position remained unchanged, the astonished justices ordered that the full amount be placed in an interest-bearing escrow account, available to the Lakota whenever they wished to "resolve the question" by withdrawing the money and pronouncing the issue "settled." The Yellow Thunder occupation began a few months later.

By now, the amount in the Black Hills settlement account is said to have grown to something over $500 million. To my knowledge, although their destitution remains every bit as dire today as thirty years ago, no Lakota has ever sought to withdraw so much as a penny of these funds. In their view, the Black Hills are no more for sale now than they were in 1975, or in 1877, when the great Oglala resistance leader, Crazy Horse, observed that "one does not sell the land upon which the people walk." As it has been, so it remains, and so it will be until the unrelinquished rights of the people are once again respected. The Yellow Thunder occupation was important in laying the groundwork for one aspect of how this will be accomplished, but the perseverance of the people themselves provides the bedrock upon which all future actions are based.

NOBLE RED MAN

Throughout the Yellow Thunder occupation, those of us at the Hills maintained a continuous interaction with the Oglala Lakota living on the nearby Pine Ridge reservation, especially such elders as the traditional Oglala
headman and spiritual leader (Frank) Fools Crow and his assistant Mathew
King, who'd been instrumental in guiding the actions of Dakota AIM since
the period leading up to the 1973 siege at Wounded Knee. While each of
them was endowed with a highly-refined bitterness of wit, Mathew in particular was gifted with a natural flair for satire, wielding it like a surgeon's
scalpel to deflate balloonfuls of Euro-supremacist presumption. When
signing official documents, for instance, he refused to inscribe anything
other than "Noble Red Man," telling anyone foolish enough to wonder that
this was the "pen name" assigned him by a multitude of his self-anointed
"Great White Fathers."

Whenever we were on the reservation, those of us from Yellow Thunder stopped off as a matter of course at the homes of whichever elders we
were nearest—Pine Ridge is a big place, so geography largely dictated who
was visited on a given day—to perform whatever chores needed doing. One
afternoon in late July 1982, several of us dropped in on Mathew on our way
back to the *tiospaye* (encampment) from a meeting with some young people
in the reservation town of Kyle and, after fetching water for his horses and
some other odds and ends, joined him under his arbor for the time-honored
social ritual of sharing coffee, cigarettes, and conversation.

At first, as we sat around swapping jokes and indulging in what amount-
ed to the AIM equivalent of gossip, there was little to distinguish the occasion
from any number of others spent relaxing in the shade of the same or similar
arbors, less still that it would mark itself indelibly upon my memory. Then
Mathew cleared his throat, indicating that there was something serious he
wished to say. He began by informing us that while he didn't question—
in fact, admired—our courage, we caused him great sadness. This was, he
said, because it was clear to him that no matter how fiercely we fought, and
no matter how long and hard we struggled, no matter how much pain we

were willing to endure, we'd been beaten before we started. Worst of all, he summed up, was that we'd, to all intents and purposes, beaten ourselves.

Having thus captured our undivided attention, as he knew he would, Mathew went on to explain why this was so, framing the problem with a clarity and straightforward elegance that, to the best of my ability, is reconstructed here.

> Anybody can see that you're filled with anger. Your anger is from the heart, and there's every reason for it, so you're right to be angry. Anybody who sees what's happening to our people should be angry about it. It's good that you feel the fire of anger burning in your bellies because that's what gives you the strength to do what you're doing, and what you're doing has to be done if the suffering of the people is ever going to end. But anger, no matter how natural and necessary, is never enough. It's true that it's made you into fighters and that fighters are needed, but you must always remember what you're fighting *for*, not just what you're fighting *against*. You understand that changes have to be made in the way things are—that's why you've chosen to fight—but it's just as important to know what *kind* of changes you're trying to bring about.
>
> That's where you're lost. You know pretty well what it is that you're trying to get away from, or at least you think you do, but you've really got no idea where you're trying to go, or how to get there. And that's why you're bound to lose.

The old man sat quietly for a few moments, allowing time for what had been said to settle in before returning his theme.

> Think of it as a journey. You want to go somewhere. To get there, you can't just head off. You have to ride in a particu-

lar direction. But, in order to know what that direction is, you have to know where you are when you set out. And you have to know where you are all along the way if you're going to be sure you haven't drifted off course. Otherwise, you might just ride forever and never get where you want to go. Chances are, you'll end up riding around in circles.

People ask me, "King, what's the best way to know where you are?" They expect me to tell them something about how the Lakota could always tell by the sun and the stars. And it's true that we know how to guide ourselves that way. But sometimes it's cloudy and you can't see the sun or the stars. So that's not the best way. What you do—and you boys know this as well as I do—you pass a landmark—a bluff, a big tree, something that sticks up—and then when you're out there moving across these plains, every once in a while you look back over your shoulder to see where you are in relation to that point. That's the best way to make sure you never get lost. Often, it's the *only* way. So you see, to know how to get to where you want to go, you have to first know where you are, and to know where you are, you always have to know where you've been. You can't do without all three of those pieces. If you're missing any one of them, you're going to be lost.

He sat back again, lit a cigarette while studying our faces, then resumed.

There are different kinds of journeys, and you boys have set out on one. You've got yourselves a big problem, though. You don't know where it is you're trying to go—not really, because "someplace else" isn't much of a destination—so you don't quite know which direction to take to get there. And that's because you're not all that clear about where you are. Oh, you know for sure that it's someplace you don't like, but if I asked you to tell me why that is, you couldn't even do *that* very well.

The reason all those things are true is because you don't know where you've been. What I'm saying is that, other than little dribs and drabs, maybe, you don't know your history. You don't really know where you're coming from. So you don't know how things were or how they got to be the way they are. That means you can't truly understand the situation you're in, not even the real nature of who and what you think you're fighting against. Since you don't really know your enemy, you can't see what must be done to defeat him or heal the pain he's caused.

You're good boys. You mean well, and you fight hard. But if you don't know your history, you're bound to just keep heading off in the wrong direction or riding around and around in circles. If you don't know your history, you'll always be beat before you start.

I later came across someone, by my recollection it was Michel Foucault, who managed to offer pretty much the same insights in about 30,000 words. There have been others, but Mathew King, the Noble Red Man, said it best. His words sparked such an epiphany in me that I've been deeply immersed in the learning of history ever since. It is a process which has involved not merely the absorption of information, but the exposure of an elaborate matrix of lies with which the triumphalist narratives of mainstream historiography have been assembled, thus countering the false consciousness thereby engendered with interpretations of the record that hew far closer to the reality of what has transpired since the predator's arrival on American shores in 1492.

In doing so, I've sought to comply with Philip Deere's enjoinders to always call things by their right names—for example, genocide is genocide; it is *not* and never was "ethnocide" or "ethnic cleansing" or whatever euphemism the perpetrators and their descendant beneficiaries may select to mask or mitigate the nature of the crime—and never to compromise the truth as I understand it (as one of my critics recently observed, "He doesn't censor himself—*at all*"). The validity of my approach, gleaned as it was from Mathew King, Philip Deere, and others of their caliber, can reasonably be measured in the magnitude of the outrage and denial my reliance upon it has generated among "responsible" academics of all flavors, manifested most notably in the sheer determination of their effort to discredit my work over the past five years.

I take immense pride in having been, and still being, the focus of such repressive animus, secure in the knowledge that to have been deemed worthy of it I must have gotten too many things right and communicated them too effectively. In the process, I've become a far more capable fighter than I was in 1982, and, hopefully, have helped others to become such as well. In this regard, my hopes are in no sense reserved for Native people. While I've always spoken from an explicitly Native standpoint, what I've had to say has always been framed in a manner intended to resonate with and be of utility to not only Native people, but those of African, Asian, and European heritage as well.

To some extent, the breadth of the audience I've sought and seek to address arises from my personal background, given that I'm of European as well as American Indian ancestry—and most likely a dash of African as well—married to a Eurasian woman, and the adoptive father of a young woman embodying an admixture of all four racial strains. More significantly, however, the breadth of my focus has resulted from an admonition from Philip, echoed by Vine Deloria and others along the way, to always remember that these others are, if anything, even more confused than we, even more in need of learning the actualities of their histories on this land and thus the true nature of our mutual present.

It is no less important that they be enabled to arrive at this clarity than that it be attained by our own youth and future generations. They, no less than we, are not only here, but will remain so. Whatever is to be done, we must ultimately do it together, not as interchangeable elements within some purportedly homogeneous social mass, but from our respective stations within a polyverse of autochthonous societies continuously interacting on the basis of common need and mutual respect. This requires that the truth of our interactive history be known and acted upon by all who profess a desire for a future better than our collective past. Only thus can the trajectory connecting where we were to where we are be altered in a manner that takes us where we want and need to go.

500 Years of Resistance

All of which takes me back to Gord Hill and the work of history he offers in this book. If it seems that I've devoted too much of the space earmarked for the introduction of *his* material to recounting certain of my own experiences and explaining why my own work has assumed the form that it has, it is because I can imagine no better means by which to at once reveal the context within which I see his *500 Years of Resistance* as taking its rightful place and the reasons why I believe this to be cause for celebration.

Despite our obvious differences, not only culturally but in terms of age and expressive media, our work is, to my mind, complementary. Another and perhaps more useful descriptor would be "confluent." We seek to connect the same historical dots, he and I, thereby demonstrating how the attitudes and behaviors displayed by US troops on the Great Plains during the 1870s link up directly with those of Spain's conquistadors 350 years earlier, for example, and how the unity of these historical actualities is ongoing in the hemisphere's proliferation of Euro-derivative settler states.

Concomitantly, we share the objective of laying bare the linkages between, say, the Mapuche resistance to colonization and genocide in Chile during the sixteenth century and that manifested in the upper Sonora desert during the 1680 Pueblo Revolt and, subsequently, in the protracted guerrilla warfare waged by the Chiricahua and other Apache peoples, as well as other early Indigenous struggles with those of AIM at Wounded Knee in 1973 (and during the Yellow Thunder occupation), the Mohawk Warriors at Oka, the Zapatistas in Chiapas, the Warriors defending Secwepmac rights at Ts'peten in 1995, and so on.

As I suggest above, Gord has perfected a method of combining graphic and written narrative that allows him to present a sweeping view of history, not only with impeccable accuracy, but very concisely and with extraordinary impact. This lends his material an equally extraordinary accessibility, thereby making "the Big Picture" available—yes, the pun *was* intended—to *anyone* willing and physically able to look at it. My own approach to the same subject matter inherently precludes my work from attaining anything resembling the same reach. (On the other hand, his method precludes the inclusion of considerable detail.)

Hence, in the spirit of synthesizing the "the best of both worlds"—the pun was again intended, although this time on multiple levels—I've decided to wrap up my contribution to Gord's book with an extensive, though by no means exhaustive, list of recommended readings. Notwithstanding my lengthy stint as a professor, this implies *no* expectation on my part, and surely not on Gord's, that anyone engaging *500 Years of Resistance* will—or even should—set themselves the goal of plowing through everything on the list. Rather, it is offered as a guide for readers wishing to further explore particular points he or I have touched upon if they wish to find more in-depth information.

RECOMMENDED READINGS

Acuña, Rodolfo. *Occupied America: The Chicano's Struggle Toward Liberation.* San Francisco: Canfield Press, 1972.

Adams, Howard. *Prison of Grass: Canada from the Native Point of View.* Toronto: New Press, 1975.

_____. *A Tortured People: The Politics of Colonialism.* Penticton, BC: Theytus Books, 1995.

Anaya, S. James. *Indigenous Peoples in International Law.* New York: Oxford University Press, 1996.

Arden, Harvey. *Noble Red Man: Lakota Wisdomkeeper Mathew King.* Hillsboro, OR: Beyond Words, 1994.

Asch, Michael. *Home and Native Land: Aboriginal Rights and the Canadian Constitution.* Vancouver: University of British Columbia Press, 1993.

_____, ed. *Aboriginal and Treaty Rights in Canada: Essays on Law, Equality, and Respect for Difference.* Vancouver: University of British Columbia Press, 1997.

Berger, Thomas R. *A Long and Terrible Shadow: White Values, Native Rights in the Americas, 1492-1992.* Vancouver: Douglas & McIntyre, 1991.

Brooks, James, ed. *Confounding the Color Line: The Indian-Black Experience in North America.* Lincoln: University of Nebraska Press, 2002.

Carew, Jan. *Rape of Paradise: Columbus and the Birth of Racism in America.* Brooklyn: A&B Books, 1994.

Axelrod, Alan. *Chronicle of the Indian Wars: From Colonial Times to Wounded Knee.* New York: Prentice Hall, 1993.

Churchill, Ward. *From a Native Son: Selected Essays in Indigenism, 1985-1995.* Cambridge, MA: South End Press, 1996.

_____. *A Little Matter of Genocide: Holocaust and Denial in the Americas, 1492 to the Present.* San Francisco: City Lights, 1997.

_____. *Fantasies of the Master Race: Literature, Cinema, and the Colonization of American Indians,* 2nd ed. San Francisco: City Lights, 1998.

_____. *Struggle for the Land: Native North American Resistance to Genocide, Ecocide and Colonization.* San Francisco: City Lights, 2002.

_____. *Perversions of Justice: Indigenous Peoples and Anglo-American Law.* San Francisco: City Lights, 2003.

_____. *Acts of Rebellion: The Ward Churchill Reader*. New York: Routledge, 2003.

_____. *Kill the Indian, Save the Man: The Genocidal Impact of Indian Residential Schools*. San Francisco: City Lights, 2004.

_____. *Since Predator Came: Notes from the Struggle for American Indian Liberation*, 2nd ed. Oakland, CA: AK Press, 2005.

Clark, Bruce. *Native Liberty, Crown Sovereignty: The Existing Aboriginal Right of Self-Government in Canada*. Montréal: McGill-Queens University Press, 1990.

Clarke, John Henrik. *Christopher Columbus and the Afrikan Holocaust: Slavery and the Rise of European Capitalism*. Brooklyn: A&B Publishers Group, 1993.

Cocker, Mark. *Rivers of Blood, Rivers of Gold: Europe's Conquest of Indigenous Peoples*. New York: Grove Press, 1998.

Deloria, Vine Jr. *Behind the Trail of Broken Treaties: An American Indian Declaration of Independence*, 2nd ed. Austin: University of Texas Press, 1985.

_____. *Custer Died for Your Sins: An Indian Manifesto*, 2nd ed. Norman: University of Oklahoma Press, 1988).

_____. *Red Earth, White Lies: Native Americans and the Myth of Scientific Fact*. New York: Scribner, 1995.

Drinnon, Richard. *Facing West: The Metaphysics of Indian-Hating and Empire-Building*. Minneapolis: University of Minnesota Press, 1980.

Durham, Jimmie. *A Certain Lack of Coherence: Writings on Art and Cultural Politics*. London: Kala Press, 1993.

Falla, Ricardo. *Massacres in the Jungle: Ixcán, Guatemala, 1975-1982*. Boulder, CO: Westview Press, 1994.

Forbes, Jack D. *Africans and Native Americans: The Language of Race and the Evolution of Red-Black Peoples*, 2nd ed. Urbana: University of Illinois Press, 1993.

_____. *Columbus and Other Cannibals*, rev. ed. New York: Seven Stories Press, 2008.

Foerstel, Lenora, ed. *Creating Surplus Populations: The Effect of Military and Corporate Policies on Indigenous Peoples*. Washington, DC: Maisonneuve Press, 1996.

Francis, Daniel. *The Imaginary Indian: The Image of the Indian in Canadian Culture*. Vancouver: Arsenal Pulp Press, 1992.

Galeano, Eduardo. *Open Veins of Latin America: Five Centuries of the Pillage of a Continent*, anniversary ed. New York: Monthly Review Press, 1997.

Garroutte, Eva Marie. *Real Indians: Identity and the Survival of American Indians*.

Berkeley: University of California Press, 2003.

Goodleaf, Donna. *Entering the War Zone: A Mohawk Perspective on Resisting Invasions*. Penticton, BC: Theytus Books, 1995.

Green, L.C., and Olive P. Dickason. *The Law of Nations and the New World*. Edmonton: University of Alberta Press, 1989.

Grenier, John. *The First Way of War: American War Making on the Frontier, 1607-1814*. Cambridge, UK: Cambridge University Press, 2005.

Hall, Anthony J. *The American Empire and the Fourth World: The Bowl with One Spoon*. Montréal: McGill-Queen's University Press, 2004.

Harring, Sidney L. *Crow Dog's Case: American Indian Sovereignty, Tribal Law, and United States Law in the Nineteenth Century*. Cambridge, UK: Cambridge University Press, 1994.

Hemming, John. *The Conquest of the Incas*. New York: Harcourt, Brace, Jovanovich, 1970.

_____. *Red Gold: The Conquest of the Brazilian Indians, 1500-1760*. Cambridge, MA: Harvard University Press, 1978.

Johnson, Troy, Joane Nagel, and Duane Champagne, eds. *American Indian Activism: Alcatraz to the Longest Walk*. Urbana: University of Illinois Press, 1997.

Katzenberger, Elaine, ed. *First World, Ha-Ha-Ha! The Zapatista Challenge*. San Francisco: City Lights, 1995.

Keal, Paul. *European Conquest and the Rights of Indigenous Peoples: The Moral Backwardness of International Society*. Cambridge, UK: Cambridge University Press, 2003.

Leon-Portilla, Miguel, ed. *The Broken Spears: The Aztec Account of the Conquest of Mexico*. Boston: Beacon Press, 1962.

Lobo, Susan, and Steve Talbot, eds. *Native American Voices: A Reader*. New York: Longman, 1998.

Lowes, Warren. *Indian Giver: A Legacy of North American Native Peoples*. Penticton, BC: Theytus Books, 1986.

Mann, Barbara Alice. *George Washington's War on Native America*. Westport, CT: Praeger, 2005.

_____. *The Tainted Gift: The Disease Method of Frontier Expansion*. Westport, CT: Praeger, 2010.

Manuel, George, and Michael Poslins. *The Fourth World: An Indian Reality*. New York: Free Press, 1974.

Matthiessen, Peter. *In the Spirit of Crazy Horse: The Story of Leonard Peltier*, 2nd ed. New York: Viking Press, 1992.

Means, Russell, with Marvin J. Wolf. *Where White Men Fear to Tread: The Autobiography of Russell Means*. New York: St. Martin's Press, 1995.

Milloy, John S. *"A National Crime": The Canadian Government and the Residential School System, 1879-1986*. Winnipeg: University of Manitoba Press, 1999.

Neitschmann, Bernard. *The Unknown War: The Miskito Nation, Nicaragua, and the United States*. Lanham, MD: Freedom House, 1989.

Neu, Dean, and Richard Therrien. *Accounting for Genocide: Canada's Bureaucratic Assault on Aboriginal People*. London: Zed Books, 2003.

Pagden, Anthony. *Lords of all the World: Ideologies of Empire in Spain, Britain and France, c. 1500-c. 1800*. New Haven: Yale University Press, 1995.

Pertusati, Linda. *In Defense of Mohawk Land: Ethnopolitical Conflict in North America*. Albany: SUNY Press, 1997.

Ross, John. *Rebellion from the Roots: Indian Uprising in the Garden*. Monroe, ME: Common Courage Press, 1995.

_____. *The War Against Oblivion: The Zapatista Chronicles*. Monroe, ME: Common Courage Press, 2000.

Saito, Natsu Taylor. *Meeting the Enemy: American Exceptionalism and International Law*. New York: New York University Press, 2010.

Sale, Kirkpatrick. *The Conquest of Paradise: Columbus and the Columbia Legacy*. New York: Alfred A. Knopf, 1990.

Smith, Andrea. *Conquest: Sexual Violence and American Indian Genocide*. Cambridge, MA: South End Press, 2005.

Smith, Linda Tuhiwai. *Decolonizing Methodologies: Research and Indigenous Peoples*. London: Zed Books, 1999.

Stannard, David E. *American Holocaust: Columbus and the Conquest of the New World*. New York: Oxford University Press, 1992.

Steele, Ian K. *Warpaths: Invasions of North America*. New York: Oxford University Press, 1994.

Switlo, Janice G.A.E. *Gustafsen Lake Under Siege*. Peachland, BC: TIAC Communications, 1997.

Tierney, Patrick. *Darkness in El Dorado: How Scientists and Journalists Devastated the Amazon*. New York: W.W. Norton, 2000.

Tinker, George E. *Missionary Conquest: The Gospel and Native American Cultural*

Genocide. Minneapolis: Fortress Press, 1993.

_____. *Spirit and Resistance: Political Theology and American Indian Liberation.* Minneapolis: Fortress Press, 2004.

_____. *American Indian Liberation: A Theology of Sovereignty.* Maryknoll, NY: Orbis Books, 2008.

Todorov, Tzvetan. *The Conquest of America.* New York: Harper Colophon, 1985.

Weyler, Rex. *Blood of the Land: The Government and Corporate War Against First Nations.* Gabriola Island, BC: New Society, 1992.

Williams, Robert A. Jr. *The American Indian in Western Legal Thought: The Discourses of Conquest.* New York: Oxford University Press, 1990.

_____. *Linking Arms Together: American Indian Treaty Visions of Law and Peace, 1600-1800.* New York: Routledge, 1999.

_____. *Like a Loaded Weapon: The Rehnquist Court, Indian Rights, and the Legal History of Racism in America.* Minneapolis: University of Minnesota Press, 2005.

York, Geoffrey, and Loreen Pindera. *People of the Pines: The Warriors and the Legacy of Oka.* Toronto: Little, Brown Canada, 1991.

1492: INVASION!

ON OCTOBER 12, 1492, THREE SPANISH SHIPS UNDER THE COMMAND OF CHRISTOPHER COLUMBUS ARRIVED IN THE AMERICAS. HIS MISSION WAS TO MAP A TRANS-ATLANTIC ROUTE TO ASIA; HE HAD NO IDEA THE 'AMERICAS' EXISTED...

INSTEAD OF ASIA, COLUMBUS LANDED IN THE CARIBBEAN, NEAR PUERTO RICO.

COLUMBUS SAW THIS AS WEAKNESS. THE TAINO AS STUPID CHILDREN WITHOUT A CULTURE, FIT TO BE CONQUERED, ENSLAVED, AND CHRISTIANIZED...

BELIEVING HE WAS NEAR THE INDIAN OCEAN, COLUMBUS NAMED THE REGION THE 'WEST INDIES', ITS PEOPLE 'INDIANS'.

THE FIRST 'INDIANS' HE MET WERE TAINOS, WHO GREETED THE SHIPS AS GUESTS. HE MADE NOTE OF THEIR GENEROSITY (AS WELL AS THEIR USE OF GOLD...).

TO THIS END HE ERECTED CROSSES ON THE ISLANDS WHERE HE LANDED, CLAIMING THEM FOR THE SPANISH CROWN AND THE CHRISTIAN EMPIRE ITSELF...

BUT THIS FIRST VOYAGE WAS JUST A RECON. THE FIRST COLONY ~ LA NAVIDAD ~ WAS THE RESULT OF A SHIP-WRECK...

PLANKS FROM THE WRECK WERE USED TO BUILD THE FORT, ON THE ISLAND OF HISPANIOLA (NOW HAITI/DOMINICAN REPUBLIC).

IN JANUARY 1493, COLUMBUS RETURNED TO SPAIN, LEAVING 40 MEN AT LA NAVIDAD WITH ORDERS TO COLLECT GOLD...

IN THE FALL OF 1493, COLUMBUS RETURNED WITH AN INVASION FORCE OF 17 SHIPS AND 1,500 COLONISTS + SOLDIERS...

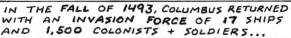

HE FOUND LA NAVIDAD DESTROYED AFTER THE TAINO RETALIATED AGAINST RAPES AND MURDERS CARRIED OUT BY THE SPANIARDS.

AGAINST EUROPEAN WEAPONS (CANNONS, MUSKETS, CROSS-BOWS, AND SWORDS), ARMOUR, HORSES, + DOGS, INDIGENOUS WARRIORS WERE POORLY EQUIPPED, ARMED MOSTLY WITH CLUBS AND SPEARS.

AS PART OF HIS COMMISSION, COLUMBUS WAS MADE GOVERNOR OF THE COLONY...

HIS JOB WAS TO FIND GOLD, ESTABLISH SETTLEMENTS, AND 'CHRISTIANIZE' THE NATIVES...

NOW A REIGN OF TERROR AND DEATH WOULD BE UNLEASHED. EVERY NATIVE OVER 14 WAS FORCED TO SUPPLY GOLD; THOSE WHO FAILED HAD THEIR HANDS AND NOSES CUT OFF...

BY FAR THE GREATEST KILLER ~ WHICH DESTROYED ANY POTENTIAL FOR RESISTANCE, WERE EUROPEAN DISEASES, WHICH CAUSED THE DEATHS OF MILLIONS OF INDIGENOUS PEOPLES...

TORTURE, RAPE, AND MURDER BECAME A DAILY ROUTINE FOR SETTLERS + SOLDIERS. ENTIRE VILLAGES WERE ENSLAVED, OR MASSACRED.

FROM 1492 TO 1514 (20 YEARS), THE TAINO DROPPED FROM 8 MILLION TO JUST 28,000.

DESPITE FORCED LABOUR + EXPORTING SLAVES, THE COLONY FAILED TO MAKE A PROFIT; SETTLERS BEGAN TO REVOLT...

IN 1500, COLUMBUS WAS SENT BACK TO SPAIN IN CHAINS. IN 1502, HE WAS RELEASED; HE RETURNED TO THE AMERICAS...

NEAR JAMAICA, HIS SHIPS BECAME SO INFESTED WITH WORMS HE WAS FORCED TO LAND AND WAS MAROONED FOR A YEAR.

IN 1504, HE WAS RESCUED. IN 1506, COLUMBUS DIED IN SPAIN, POSSIBLY FROM A DISEASE CAUGHT IN THE AMERICAS.

FROM THE CARIBBEAN, THE SPANISH EXPANDED INTO CENTRAL + SOUTH AMERICA, CONFRONTING LARGE NATIVE EMPIRES.

FROM 1517-1521, THE SPANISH ATTACKED THE MEXICA (AZTEC) IN CENTRAL MEXICO. THEY WERE JOINED BY 20-30,000 WARRIORS FROM NATIONS THAT HAD BEEN CONQUERED BY THE MEXICA...

IN PERU, THE INCA WERE ALSO QUICKLY DEFEATED (FROM 1531-1533) BY A SMALL GROUP OF CONQUISTADORS...

BOTH EMPIRES FELL DUE TO INTERNAL DIVISIONS, WAR, + DISEASE. IN PERU, MEXICO + BOLIVIA, HUGE GOLD + SILVER MINES WERE BUILT; MILLIONS OF NATIVE SLAVES WERE WORKED TO DEATH...

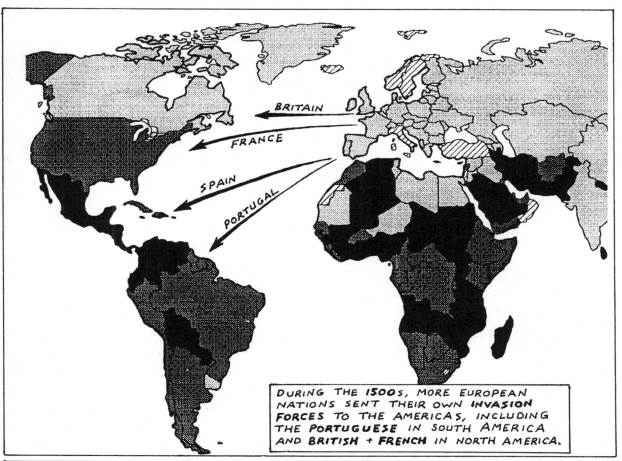

DURING THE **1500**s, MORE EUROPEAN NATIONS SENT THEIR OWN **INVASION FORCES** TO THE AMERICAS, INCLUDING THE **PORTUGUESE** IN SOUTH AMERICA AND **BRITISH + FRENCH** IN NORTH AMERICA.

AT THIS TIME, EUROPE WAS **SUFFERING** FROM **POVERTY, FAMINE, DISEASE, AND WAR...**

THE **COLONIZATION** OF THE AMERICAS MADE EUROPE **WEALTHY;** GOLD, SILVER, WOOD + FOOD CROPS POURED IN ~ **STOLEN** FROM **INDIGENOUS** LANDS AND **ENSLAVEMENT.**

IN NORTH AMERICA THERE WAS LITTLE GOLD OR SILVER AND LONG, COLD WINTERS. EARLY SETTLERS RELIED ON INDIGENOUS PEOPLE FOR SURVIVAL + ECONOMIC TRADE.

THE FIRST ENGLISH COLONY WAS SET UP IN 1607 IN PRESENT-DAY 'VIRGINIA'.

BY THE 1620s THERE WAS WIDESPREAD FIGHTING AS SETTLERS TOOK MORE AND MORE LAND...

ENTIRE VILLAGES WERE MASSACRED AND THEIR CROPS TAKEN BY THE SETTLERS.

THEY PAID MONEY FOR NATIVE SCALPS —ALL TO KILL THE PEOPLE AND TAKE THEIR LAND!

SOON, TENS OF THOUSANDS OF EUROPEAN SETTLERS WERE IN EASTERN N. AMERICA.

BUYING AND SELLING STOLEN INDIGENOUS LAND BECAME A BIG BUSINESS FOR AN OVER-POPULATED + LAND-HUNGRY EUROPE.

MEANWHILE, THE SPANISH + PORTUGUESE BEGAN IMPORTING INDIGENOUS AFRICANS AS SLAVES TO WORK IN THEIR COLONIES.

SOON THE SLAVE TRADE EXTENDED INTO THE BRITISH COLONIES IN N. AMERICA. OVER 30 MILLION DIED ON SLAVE SHIPS.

BY THE LATE 1600'S, THE BRITISH + FRENCH WERE AT **WAR** FOR CONTROL OF THE NORTH AMERICAN COLONIES AND A GLOBAL EMPIRE.

IN 1763 THE FRENCH WERE DEFEATED AND SURRENDERED ALL THEIR N. AMERICAN COLONIES.

THE 1763 ROYAL PROCLAMATION SET A WESTERN BOUNDARY FOR ALL SETTLERS...

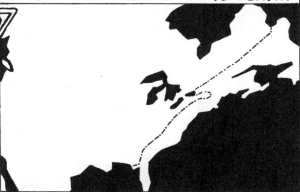

NO TRADE OR SETTLEMENT COULD OCCUR WITHOUT THE LEGAL SURRENDER OF INDIGENOUS LANDS TO THE BRITISH...

THE BRITISH NOW HAD A VAST AREA TO CONTROL, WITH HOSTILE FRENCH SETTLERS AND ONGOING INDIGENOUS RESISTANCE.

ONE RESPONSE WAS TO ISSUE A NEW LAW~ THE 1763 ROYAL PROCLAMATION.

THIS ANGERED MANY SETTLERS, ALONG WITH MORE TAXES IMPOSED BY BRITAIN.

BY 1775 MANY COLONIES UNITED AND DECLARED INDEPENDENCE FROM BRITAIN. THE 'AMERICAN REVOLUTION' HAD BEGUN.

IN 1783, THE BRITISH SURRENDERED. THE NEWLY-FORMED UNITED STATES THEN BEGAN TO EXPAND WEST, ATTACKING INDIGENOUS NATIONS. THE US 'INDIAN WARS' WOULD CONTINUE FOR 100 YEARS...

IN 1812, THE US INVADED EASTERN CANADA WHILE BRITAIN WAS AGAIN AT WAR WITH FRANCE IN EUROPE...

ONLY WITH THE AID OF AN INDIGENOUS CONFEDERACY~LED BY TECUMSEH AND BLACKHAWK~WERE U.S. FORCES REPELLED.

WHILE THESE 'REVOLUTIONS' TALKED ABOUT FREEDOM + EQUALITY, INDIGENOUS PEOPLES REMAINED UNDER MILITARY ATTACK...

BY THIS TIME, THE US 'REVOLUTION' HAD INSPIRED SPANISH SETTLERS IN S. AMERICA.

FROM 1809 TO 1821, SETTLER REVOLTS CREATED MANY NEW STATES: BOLIVIA, PERU, ARGENTINA, CHILE, VENEZUELA, AND MEXICO...

AS THE US 'INDIAN WARS' CONTINUED, THOUSANDS OF CHEROKEES DIED ON THE 'TRAIL OF TEARS' IN THE WINTER OF 1838.

ALONG WITH OTHERS, THE CHEROKEES WERE FORCIBLY RELOCATED TO OKLAHOMA.

IN 1848 THE US INVADED AND TOOK CONTROL OF NORTHERN MEXICO (NOW THE STATES OF CALIFORNIA, NEVADA, UTAH, COLORADO, ARIZONA, NEW MEXICO + TEXAS.

THAT SAME YEAR, GOLD WAS FOUND IN CALIFORNIA.

SETTLERS POURED IN, KILLING TENS OF THOUSANDS OF NATIVES. GOLD MINES ALSO KILLED MANY RIVERS...

IN THE 1860s, US FORCES BEGAN TO ATTACK THE PLAINS INDIGENOUS NATIONS (I.E., THE LAKOTA, CHEYENNE, ARAPAHO...).

AT THE SAME TIME, US TROOPS ALSO BEGAN MILITARY CAMPAIGNS TO PACIFY TRIBES IN THE SOUTHWEST...

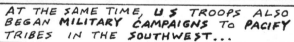

THE APACHE, NAVAJO, YAQUI, COMANCHEES, AND OTHERS WOULD FIGHT A LONG GUERRILLA WAR UNTIL THE 1880s.

ON JUNE 25, 1876, THE US MILITARY SUFFERED A HUMILIATING DEFEAT WHEN LAKOTAS + CHEYENNES DESTROYED CUSTER'S 'ELITE' 7th CALVARY, UNDER THE LEADERSHIP OF CRAZY HORSE, GALL, RED HORSE, AND OTHERS...

TO DEPRIVE THE PLAINS NATIONS OF FOOD, SHELTER, ETC., U.S FORCES ALMOST EXTERMINATED THE BUFFALO.

ON THE CANADIAN PRAIRIES, THE PEOPLE ALSO FACED HUNGER. COLONIAL AGENTS EXPLOITED THIS TO MAKE TREATIES...

THESE TREATIES SURRENDERED LARGE TRACTS OF LAND IN EXCHANGE FOR FOOD, SHELTER, AND RESERVATIONS.

IN 1876, THE SAME YEAR AS CUSTER'S DEFEAT, CANADA PASSED THE INDIAN ACT...

WITH THIS, BAND COUNCILS + RESERVES WERE IMPOSED ON NATIVES ACROSS THE COUNTRY, BACKED BY POLICE FORCE.

IN 1885, CREE + METIS WARRIORS, LED BY BIG BEAR + LOUIS RIEL, REBELLED AGAINST GOVERNMENT CONTROL IN SOUTH MANITOBA.

DEFEATED BY THOUSANDS OF TROOPS, THIS WAS THE LAST ARMED RESISTANCE IN THE COLONIZATION OF CANADA.

IN 1890, TROOPERS OF THE REFORMED 7TH CALVARY MASSACRED SOME 300 LAKOTAS, MANY WOMEN + CHILDREN, AT WOUNDED KNEE, SOUTH DAKOTA.

THIS MARKED THE END OF INDIGENOUS MILITARY RESISTANCE TO COLONIZATION. NOW THE SYSTEMATIC ASSIMILATION OF NATIVE PEOPLES WOULD BEGIN...

• END OF PART ONE •

PART 2: RESISTANCE!

THE COLONIZATION OF THE AMERICAS BY EUROPEAN FORCES WAS NOT EASY. IT INVOLVED CENTURIES OF WAR AS OUR ANCESTORS FOUGHT A LIFE + DEATH STRUGGLE.

THE RESISTANCE BEGAN ALMOST IMMEDIATELY WITH THE TAINO ATTACK ON THE FIRST COLONY~ LA NAVIDAD ~ IN 1493...

MEXICO

THE FORT WAS DESTROYED AND 40 SPANIARDS KILLED...

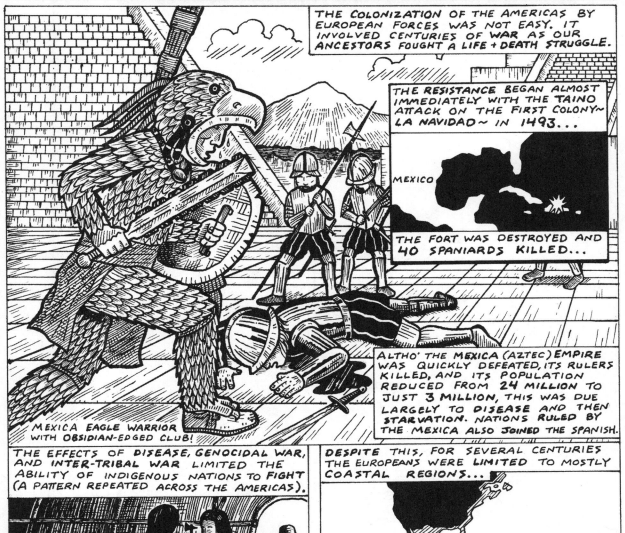

MEXICA EAGLE WARRIOR WITH OBSIDIAN-EDGED CLUB!

ALTHO' THE MEXICA (AZTEC) EMPIRE WAS QUICKLY DEFEATED, ITS RULERS KILLED, AND ITS POPULATION REDUCED FROM 24 MILLION TO JUST 3 MILLION, THIS WAS DUE LARGELY TO DISEASE AND THEN STARVATION. NATIONS RULED BY THE MEXICA ALSO JOINED THE SPANISH.

THE EFFECTS OF DISEASE, GENOCIDAL WAR, AND INTER-TRIBAL WAR LIMITED THE ABILITY OF INDIGENOUS NATIONS TO FIGHT (A PATTERN REPEATED ACROSS THE AMERICAS).

DESPITE THIS, FOR SEVERAL CENTURIES THE EUROPEANS WERE LIMITED TO MOSTLY COASTAL REGIONS...

EUROPEAN COLONIAL FORCES 1492-1700

THEY WERE LIMITED BY FACTORS SUCH AS TERRAIN, WEATHER (IN THE NORTH), DISEASE (IN THE SOUTH) AND RESISTANCE.

INCA INSURGENCY
FROM 1500S TO TÚPAC AMARU, 1780S

THE INCA WERE A LARGE CIVILIZATION IN PRESENT-DAY PERU WHEN THE SPANISH INVASION BEGAN IN THE 1530S.

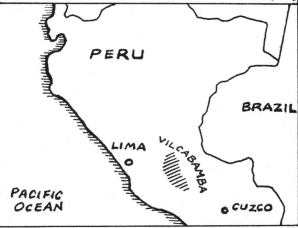

THE SPANISH KILLED THE INCA RULER & EXPLOITED DISEASE & INTERNAL DIVISION TO QUICKLY GAIN CONTROL.

AT THIS TIME, MANCO INCA AND THE RESISTANCE WITHDREW TO THE MOUNTAINS & JUNGLES OF VILCABAMBA.

IN 1536, MANCO INCA LED A REVOLT THAT LAID SIEGE TO LIMA & CUZCO, KILLING MANY 'CONQUISTADORS'...

AT CUZCO, A SIEGE WENT ON FOR 1 YEAR ALTHO' OTHER REGIONS REBELLED, THE INCA ARMY COULD NOT DRIVE OUT THE WELL-ARMED SPANISH FORCES.

FOR 30 YEARS, THE INCA RESISTED FROM THEIR LIBERATED ZONE UNTIL SPANISH & NATIVE MERCENARIES OVERTOOK VILCABAMBA, IN 1572.

FROM 1780-83, THE 'LAST INCA REVOLT' OCCURRED, SPREADING FROM PERU TO ECUADOR, COLOMBIA, AND BOLIVIA...

TÚPAC AMARU II HELPED LEAD REBELS AGAINST CORRUPTION, SLAVERY, HUNGER & OPPRESSIVE TAXES...

AFTER PLANNING & ORGANIZING, THE REBELLION WAS LAUNCHED IN 1780.

THE INSURGENTS CAPTURED TOWNS, KILLING COLONIAL OFFICIALS, SOLDIERS, PRIESTS & SETTLERS.

IN BOLIVIA, TÚPAC KATARI LED REBELS IN A SIEGE OF **LA PAZ**. OF ITS **20,000** INHABITANTS, OVER **ONE-THIRD** DIED.

IN MAY 1781, TÚPAC AMARU WAS CAPTURED & KILLED. AFTER HIS DEATH, THE INSURGENCY INTENSIFIED.

BY 1783, HOWEVER, THE LAST OF THE REBEL FORCES WERE DEFEATED AND THEIR LEADERS KILLED. TODAY, TÚPAC AMARU & TÚPAC KATARI CONTINUE TO INSPIRE RESISTANCE.

THE UNCONQUERED MAPUCHE

THE MAPUCHE OF SOUTHERN CHILE RESISTED THE SPANISH FOR THREE CENTURIES & WERE NEVER CONQUERED. THEY STILL RESIST CHILE TODAY.

IN THE 1520s, THE SPANISH BEGAN TO INVADE THE NORTHERN REGION.

IN 1541, THE CAPITAL OF SANTIAGO WAS ESTABLISHED, BUT DESTROYED WITHIN MONTHS BY MAPUCHE WARRIORS.

IN 1553, A MAPUCHE YOUTH ~ LAUTARO ~ ESCAPED HIS ENSLAVEMENT TO THE COLONIAL GOVERNOR, PEDRO VALDIVIA.

LAUTARO HAD LEARNED SPANISH & WEAPONS. WHEN HE RETURNED TO HIS PEOPLE, HE HELPED THEM ORGANIZE.

LAUTARO BECAME A LEADER IN THE MAPUCHE GUERRILLA WAR AGAINST THE SPANISH. HE TAUGHT NEW STRATEGIES, INCL. THE USE OF HORSES.

IN DECEMBER 1553, MAPUCHES LED BY LAUTARO ATTACKED CONCEPCION, A SPANISH FORT. VALDIVIA HIMSELF LED A LARGE FORCE OF REINFORCEMENTS.

THEY WERE AMBUSHED AND WIPED OUT. VALDIVIA WAS CAPTURED & LATER KILLED.

LAUTARO CONTINUED FIGHTING, UNTIL HE WAS KILLED IN BATTLE IN 1557.

THE MAPUCHE CONTINUED TO RESIST THE SPANISH, UNTIL CHILE GAINED ITS INDEPENDENCE, IN 1818.

EVEN AFTER CHILE'S INDEPENDENCE, THE MAPUCHE FOUGHT TO DEFEND THEIR LAND UNTIL 1882, WHEN THEY WERE FINALLY DEFEATED...

THEY WERE PLACED ON SOME 2,500 RESERVES. TODAY, THE MAPUCHE NUMBER SOME 1 MILLION, AND ARE STILL DEFENDING THEIR LANDS!

1680 PUEBLO REVOLT

IN THE 1590s, THE SPANISH BEGAN EXPANDING NORTH, FROM MEXICO TO WHAT IS NOW THE U S SOUTHWEST.

THEY SET UP 'NEW MEXICO,' STEALING NATIVE LAND + CROPS + ENSLAVING MANY. ALL CULTURE WAS BANNED.

IN 1675, NEARLY 50 TEWA WERE FOUND GUILTY OF 'WITCH CRAFT.' SOME WERE HUNG, OTHERS ENSLAVED, STILL OTHERS WHIPPED + IMPRISONED...

AN ANGRY TEWA DELEGATION WENT TO SANTA FE, THE SPANISH CAPITAL. THEY DEMANDED THEIR PEOPLE BE FREED.

THE SPANISH AUTHORITIES RELENTED. AMONG THOSE FREED WAS POPAY...

POPAY WAS ANGRY AND DETERMINED THAT THE SPANISH BE FORCED OUT.

HE + OTHERS BEGAN TO SECRETLY ORGANIZE A REBELLION. 5 YEARS LATER, THEY WERE READY...

THE UPRISING BEGAN ON AUGUST 10, 1680. PRIESTS + COLONISTS IN OUTLYING AREAS WERE KILLED, HOMES + CHURCHES BURNED.

HUNDREDS OF SETTLERS FLED TO SANTA FE, WHERE THE CITY WAS MADE READY FOR AN EXPECTED ATTACK.

SHORTLY AFTER, THE CITY WAS SUR-ROUNDED BY 2,500 WARRIORS. THEY CUT OFF THE CITY'S WATER CANAL...

ON AUGUST 15, THE ATTACK BEGAN ON THE CITY OUTSKIRTS. THE COLONISTS RETREATED TO A CENTRAL PALACE...

THEY WATCHED AS THEIR ESTATES + HOMES WERE LOOTED AND THEN BURNED.

THEN THE PALACE ITSELF WAS LAID SIEGE TO. THE SPANISH BARRICADED THEMSELVES IN. WITHOUT WATER AND LOW ON AMMO, THEIR DEFEAT WAS INEVITABLE...

FIGHTING CONTINUED FOR SEVERAL DAYS IN THE STREETS.

ON AUGUST 21, THE SURVIVING COLONISTS ESCAPED + FLED TO MEXICO. ALL TRACES OF THE SPAN-ISH + CHRISTIANITY WERE DESTROYED!

PONTIAC

1763 REBELLION AND THE ROYAL PROCLAMATION

PONTIAC WAS A WAR CHIEF OF THE OTTAWA. BORN AROUND 1720 NEAR LAKE ERIE, HE WAS A GIFTED SPEAKER, STRATEGIST, AND MILITARY COMMANDER.

IN THE 1700s, THE BRITISH + FRENCH WERE AT WAR IN BOTH EUROPE + N. AMERICA.

IN THE GREAT LAKES REGION, MANY TRIBES SIDED WITH THE FRENCH, WHO TRADED GUNS + AMMO FOR FUR; THE BRITISH WANTED NOT ONLY TRADE BUT ALSO LAND.

BY THE EARLY 1760s, THE FRENCH HAD SURRENDERED. THE BRITISH IMPOSED STRICT LIMITS ON TRADE WITH THE PEOPLE, ESPECIALLY GUNS + AMMO...

BY THIS TIME, PONTIAC WAS A RESPECTED LEADER. HE CALLED FOR WAR AGAINST THE BRITISH. AS MORE BRITISH SETTLERS INVADED, PONTIAC GAINED MORE SUPPORT.

DURING THE WINTER OF 1762-63, PONTIAC + WAR CHIEFS FROM MANY TRIBES (HURON, CHIPPEWA, POTAWATOMI, ETC.) BEGAN PLANNING THEIR OFFENSIVE...

IN MAY 1763, PONTIAC LED AN ATTACK AGAINST FORT DETROIT, A WELL-ARMED AND FORTIFIED POST. THE SIEGE WOULD LAST 7 MONTHS...

MANITOBA

LAKE SUPERIOR

FT. MICHILIMACKINAC

LAKE HURON

ONTARIO

FT. EDWARD AUGUSTUS

LAKE MICHIGAN

TORONTO

L. ONTARIO

FT. NIAGRA

FT. DETROIT

LAKE ERIE

FT. PRESQU

FT. LEBOEUF

FT. VENANGO

FT. ST. JOSEPH

FT. SANDUSKY

FT. PITT

FT. LIGONIER

100   200 MILES

1763
INDIGENOUS INSURGENCY

BY LATE JUNE, 8 OF 12 BRITISH FORTS HAD BEEN **CAPTURED**, ALONG WITH SUPPLY SHIPS AND CONVOYS.

HUNDREDS OF SOLDIERS HAD BEEN KILLED WHILE **THOUSANDS** OF SETTLERS FLED IN TERROR...

AT THIS TIME, SIR JEFFERY AMHERST, COMMANDER OF ALL BRITISH FORCES IN N. AMERICA, DIRECTED OFFICERS TO **DISTRIBUTE** BLANKETS + CLOTHING INFECTED WITH **SMALL POX**...

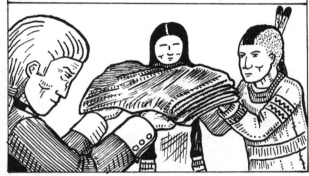

IN OCTOBER, THE BRITISH ISSUED THE 1763 ROYAL PROCLAMATION, WHICH SET A BOUNDARY LINE FOR SETTLERS AND RECOGNIZED NATIVE TITLE TO LAND.

ON OCTOBER 20, PONTIAC RECIEVED NEWS THAT THE FRENCH WOULD NOT RE-ENTER THE WAR AGAINST BRITAIN.

COMBINED, THESE FACTORS SERVED TO UNDERMINE THE INSURGENCY, AND BY NOVEMBER, LARGE NUMBERS OF WARRIORS HAD LEFT THE WAR...

IN MID-NOVEMBER, PONTIAC ENDED THE SIEGE OF FORT DETROIT. HE CONTINUED TO PROMOTE **RESISTANCE** UNTIL HIS MURDER ON APRIL 20, 1769.

SEMINOLE WARS

IN FLORIDA, SEMINOLE & ESCAPED AFRIKAN SLAVES FOUGHT TWO WARS AGAINST **U S** COLONIAL FORCES...

IN 1816, **U S** MILITIAS INVADED SOUTH FLORIDA TO ATTACK SEMINOLE & AFRIKAN VILLAGES.

MANY ESCAPED AFRIKAN SLAVES SOUGHT & FOUND SANCTUARY IN THE SWAMPS OF FLORIDA, OR AMONG THE SEMINOLE.

FLORIDA, CLAIMED BY SPAIN, BECAME A **U S** TERRITORY IN 1819, & EFFORTS TO DESTROY THE SEMINOLE INCREASED.

THEY INFLICTED MANY CASUALTIES, KILLING OVER 1,500 **U S** SOLDIERS AND COSTING UP TO $60 MILLION...

THIS LED TO THE SECOND SEMINOLE WAR (1835-42). OSCEOLA HELPED LEAD A GUERRILLA WAR AGAINST **U S** FORCES USING RAIDS, AMBUSHES, & SABOTAGE.

IN 1837, OSCEOLA WAS **BETRAYED** BY A **U S** TRUCE & IMPRISONED, DYING THE NEXT YEAR IN PRISON. ALTHO' MANY WERE **RELOCATED** TO OKLAHOMA, THE SEMINOLE REMAINED IN THEIR LANDS!

APACHE GUERRILLAS OF THE SOUTHWEST!

THE APACHES WERE A CONSTANT THREAT TO EUROPEAN COLONISTS, RAIDING SETTLEMENTS AND TAKING HORSES, WEAPONS, FOOD AND CAPTIVES. THEY WERE NEVER CONQUERED BY SPAIN OR MEXICO.

AS A RESULT OF WAR WITH MEXICO, THE US TOOK POSSESSION OF THE SOUTHWEST IN 1848...

ALTHO' APACHES CONTINUED THEIR RAIDS INTO MEXICO, THERE WAS LITTLE CONFLICT WITH AMERICAN SETTLERS...

THEN, IN 1861, COCHISE, A CHIRICAHUA APACHE, WAS CHARGED WITH RAIDING A US SETTLEMENT.

SOLDIERS TRIED TO ARREST HIM, BUT HE ESCAPED. COCHISE'S BROTHER AND NEPHEWS WERE HUNG. NOW IT WAS WAR!

COCHISE WAS JOINED BY MANGAS COLORADO. THEY CUT OFF APACHE PASS, A VITAL ROUTE TO CALIFORNIA.

IN 1862, THE CIVIL WAR SAW MANY US TROOPS MOVED EAST. A MILITIA OF 3,000 CALIFORNIA SETTLERS WAS SENT TO RE-OPEN APACHE PASS...

IN JULY 1862, OVER 500 APACHES FOUGHT THE MILITIA - BUT HAD TO RETREAT FROM THE DEADLY EFFECTS OF CANNONS.

MANGAS WAS BADLY INJURED + LATER CAPTURED + KILLED IN JANUARY 1863. MANGAS WAS OVER 70 YEARS OLD...

COCHISE + OTHERS CONTINUED FIGHTING UNTIL 1872, WHEN THEY ACCEPTED A RESERVE IN THE CHIRICAHUA MOUNTAINS.

BY THEN, MOST APACHES HAD BEEN FORCED ONTO RESERVES. IN 1875, THE US RELOCATED ALL APACHES TO THE SAN CARLOS RESERVATION ON THE GILA RIVER.

MANY APACHE GROUPS RESISTED THIS IDEA, INCLUDING VICTORIO. IN 1877 HE + 300 OTHERS ESCAPED SAN CARLOS.

BEFORE HIS DEATH IN 1880, VICTORIO'S GROUP KILLED OVER 400 SETTLERS + SOLDIERS IN RAIDS + GUN BATTLES.

CONDITIONS AT SAN CARLOS PROMPTED MORE BREAK-OUTS, INCLUDING ONE LED BY GERONIMO (GOYOKLA) IN 1881...

GERONIMO HAD FOUGHT WITH COCHISE + VICTORIO + WAS A SEASONED GUERRILLA.

GERONIMO'S GROUP WENT INTO MEXICO + RAIDED BOTH US + MEXICAN RANCHES. BOTH COUNTRIES AGREED THAT TROOPS CHASING APACHES COULD CROSS THE BORDER.

THE US ALSO HIRED HUNDREDS OF APACHE SCOUTS TO TRACK DOWN THOSE THAT CONTINUED TO RESIST...

IN 1884, GERONIMO SURRENDERED BUT ESCAPED AGAIN IN 1885 DUE TO THE OPPRESSIVE CONDITIONS OF THE RESERVES.

WITH 35 WARRIORS + 100 WOMEN AND CHILDREN, GERONIMO'S GROUP EVADED 5,000 US TROOPS + 400 APACHE SCOUTS FOR 6 MONTHS, KILLING NEARLY 100 SETTLERS + SOLDIERS. HE FINALLY SURRENDERED IN 1886...

GERONIMO AND OTHER 'HOSTILES' WERE TAKEN PRISONER AND SENT TO A PRISON CAMP IN FLORIDA (MANY OF THEIR FAMILIES WERE ALREADY THERE). SCORES OF APACHE SCOUTS WERE ALSO DISARMED + SENT TO PRISON IN FLORIDA.

AT THE SAME TIME, THE FIRST APACHE CHILDREN WERE SENT TO THE CARLISLE INDIAN SCHOOL IN PENNSYL-VANIA. GERONIMO REMAINED A PRISONER UNTIL HIS DEATH IN 1909.

WAR ON THE PLAINS

BY THE 1850s, THE US HAD EXPANDED INTO THE PLAINS, COMING INTO CONFLICT WITH NATIONS SUCH AS THE CHEYENNE, ARAPAHO, LAKOTA, + OTHERS...

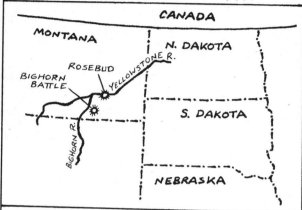

IN THE 1870s, MINERS HAD BEGUN MOVING INTO THE SACRED BLACK HILLS REGION.

AT THIS TIME, THE LAKOTA WERE ONE OF THE LARGEST PLAINS NATIONS WITH A POPULATION OF SOME 20,000...

IN 1876, THOUSANDS OF US TROOPS, LED BY GENERAL SHERIDAN, BEGAN A CAMPAIGN TO PACIFY THE LAST OF THESE 'HOSTILES'.

ON JUNE 17, 1876, A COLUMN OF 1,300 US TROOPS, WITH CROW + SHOSHONE SCOUTS, WAS CAMPED ON ROSEBUD CREEK IN MONTANA.

THEY WERE ATTACKED BY SOME 2,000 LAKOTA, CHEYENNE, AND ARAPAHO WARRIORS LED BY CRAZY HORSE, A STRANGE LAKOTA WARRIOR...

THE COLUMN, LED BY GENERAL CROOK, LOST 28 MEN, WITH 56 BADLY WOUNDED. THE INDIANS LOST 13. THE TROOPS HAD FIRED 25,000 ROUNDS. LOW ON AMMO + WITH SO MANY WOUNDED, CROOK WAS FORCED TO WITHDRAW.

ON THE LITTLE BIGHORN RIVER, AS MANY AS 15,000 INDIANS HAD GATHERED. ON JUNE 25, 1876, THE SOLDIERS WERE WITHIN STRIKING DISTANCE...

WITH SOME 2,500 TROOPS, THE CALVARY WAS CONFIDENT OF VICTORY...

GENERAL CUSTER, WITH 250 TROOPERS OF THE 'ELITE' 7TH CALVARY, WAS SENT TO LOCATE THE CAMP + AWAIT REINFORCEMENTS.

INSTEAD, HE LAUNCHED AN ATTACK, SEVERLY UNDERESTIMATING THE LARGE NUMBER OF WARRIORS (ABOUT 5,000).

CUSTER AND ALL 250 TROOPERS WERE KILLED, ONE OF THE GREATEST DEFEATS OF U S MILITARY FORCES IN HISTORY.

DESPITE THESE VICTORIES, MORE + MORE SOLDIERS CAME. THE BUFFALO WERE EXTERMINATED. MANY SURRENDERED AND ACCEPTED LIFE ON RESERVATIONS...

IN 1877, CRAZY HORSE, WITH 1,500 OTHERS, SURRENDERED, ONE OF THE LAST PLAINS GROUPS TO DO SO. ON SEPTEMBER 5, 1877, CRAZY HORSE WAS KILLED RESISTING ARREST + IMPRISONMENT.

WAR ON THE COAST

THE FIRST EUROPEANS ON THE NORTHWEST COAST WERE A 1741 RUSSIAN EXPEDITION THAT SAILED TO SOUTHERN ALASKA...

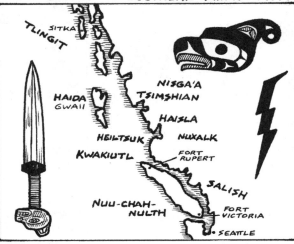

SOON, GANGS OF ARMED RUSSIANS WERE TAKING ALEUT FAMILIES HOSTAGE + FORCING HUNTERS TO GATHER SEA OTTER SKINS...

IN 1763, ALEUTS REVOLTED + DESTROYED 4 OF 5 RUSSIAN SHIPS. IN RETALIATION, MANY ALEUT VILLAGERS WERE MASSACRED.

IN 1774, A SPANISH EXPEDITION SAILED TO HAIDA GWAII. IN 1775, A SPANISH BOAT CREW WAS KILLED BY QUINAULT WARRIORS ON 'WASHINGTON'S' COAST.

IN 1778, A BRITISH NAVAL FORCE UNDER CAPT. COOK ARRIVED AT NOOTKA SOUND ON SOUTH VANCOUVER ISLAND, CLAIMING THE LANDS FOR THE BRITISH EMPIRE.

FOR SEVERAL DECADES THE FUR TRADE WAS THE MAIN CONCERN OF EUROPEAN + U S SHIPS ENTERING THE REGION...

THIS TRADE DECIMATED THE SEA OTTER POPULATION. SHIP'S CREWS USED FORCE AT TIMES TO ENSURE COMPLIANCE, EVEN TAKING HOSTAGES.

IN 1786, THE BRITISH SHIP SEA OTTER WAS ATTACKED BY NUU-CHAH-NULTH WARRIORS WHO TRIED TO SIEZE IT...

THE ATTACK WAS REPELLED BY THE CREW WITH GUN FIRE. AS MANY AS 50 WARRIORS WERE KILLED.

THROUGHOUT THE 1780s + '90s MORE EUROPEAN + U S SHIPS WERE ATTACKED. IN 1794, THE RESOLUTION WAS CAPTURED + DESTROYED BY HAIDA WARRIORS, WHO KILLED THE ENTIRE CREW...

IN 1802, A RUSSIAN FORT AT SITKA WAS DESTROYED BY AS MANY AS 1,000 TLINGIT WARRIORS. THE TLINGIT WERE WELL-ARMED THRU TRADE AND DETERMINED TO DEFEND THEIR LANDS...

IN 1803, THE U S SHIP BOSTON WAS ATTACKED BY NUU-CHAH-NULTH WARRIORS, WHO KILLED 25 OF 27 CREW MEMBERS.

THE 2 SURVIVORS WERE FORCED TO IDENT-IFY THE SEVERED HEADS OF THE CREW. THEY WERE ENSLAVED FOR 2 YEARS...

IN 1804, THE RUSSIANS RETURNED TO SITKA WITH A LARGE NAVAL FORCE...

FOR 6 DAYS THE TLINGIT RESISTED UNTIL THEY RAN LOW ON AMMO + EXPECTED REINFORCEMENTS FAILED TO ARRIVE...

RELATIONS REMAINED TENSE BETWEEN THE TLINGIT + RUSSIANS.

IN 1811, THE U S SHIP TONQUIN WAS ATTACKED BY NUU-CHAH-NULTH IN CLAYOQUOT SOUND. A FEW SURVIVING CREW MEMBERS RIGGED EXPLOSIVES + ESCAPED. THE EXPLOSION KILLED AS MANY AS 100 NUU-CHAH-NULTH.

BY THE 1820 S, THE HUDSON'S BAY COMPANY WAS THE MAIN COLONIAL POWER IN THE REGION...

THE H B C HAD NUMEROUS FORTS + SHIPS. IN 1828, A KLALLAM VILLAGE IN WASHINGTON WAS DESTROYED BY A COMPANY GUNBOAT + MILITIA...

IN 1843, FORT VICTORIA WAS BUILT BY THE HBC ON VANCOUVER ISLAND, BECOMING A MAIN CENTRE OF TRADE.

IN 1849, VANCOUVER ISLAND WAS NAMED AN OFFICIAL COLONY, WITH THE HBC ACTING AS GOVERNMENT.

AT THIS TIME, ROYAL NAVY GUNBOATS WERE BASED IN VICTORIA + PATROLLED ALONG THE COAST TO ENFORCE COLONIAL RULE.

HMS BOXER

THE GUNBOATS SERVED AS MILITARY + POLICE FORCES...

THEY WERE WELL-ARMED WITH UP TO 50 CANNONS + ROCKETS AS WELL AS ROYAL MARINES.

AT THE SAME TIME, SETTLEMENT AND SELLING LAND BECAME A MAIN CONCERN OF THE GOVERNMENT...

THE KWAKIUTL ARE STILL HEAD-HUNTING?

VANCOUVER ISLAND COLONY

YES, SIR...

FOR 30 YEARS, ROYAL NAVY GUN-BOATS WERE USED TO IMPOSE BRITISH COLONIALISM + TO BRING THE COAST TRIBES UNDER CONTROL.

IN 1850, THE NEWITTI- A KWAKIUTL GROUP - WERE ACCUSED OF KILLING SETTLERS, NEAR FORT RUPERT...

A GUNBOAT WAS SENT BUT THE NEWITTI REFUSED TO COOPERATE. MARINES WERE SENT ASHORE; THEY FOUND THE VILLAGE EMPTY + BURNED IT DOWN.

IN JULY 1851, A GUNBOAT RETURNED. NEWITTI WARRIORS OPENED FIRE + THE VILLAGE WAS BOMBARDED...

BOOM!

THE PEOPLE TOOK COVER IN THE FOREST. MARINES WENT INTO THE VILLAGE AND BURNED CANOES AND THE HOUSES...

THE NEWITTI TURNED OVER 3 DEAD, CLAIMING THESE WERE THE SUSPECTS.

THAT SAME YEAR, TLINGITS DESTROYED ANOTHER FORT, WHILE HAIDAS AND NUU-CHAH-NULTH LOOTED MORE SHIPS.

IN THE WINTER OF 1852-53, THE 'COWICHAN CRISIS' OCCURRED AFTER A SETTLER WAS KILLED.

A GUNBOAT WENT TO NANAIMO AND ARRESTED 2 SALISH WARRIORS. THE VILLAGE WAS FORCED TO GATHER + WITNESS THEIR EXECUTIONS.

IN 1856, GUNBOATS WERE AGAIN SENT AGAINST THE SALISH AT COWICHAN BAY, WHO WERE SEEN AS A THREAT. THE DEATH OF A SETTLER WAS USED TO LAUNCH A MASSIVE RAID...

...UNDER THE LAWS OF THE IMPERIAL...

500 MARINES WITH 2 CANNONS WERE DEPLOYED. THE COWICHAN SUBMITTED AND A WARRIOR WAS HUNG THE NEXT DAY IN FRONT OF THE VILLAGE.

EARLIER THAT YEAR, IN JANUARY 1856, SOME 1,000 SALISH WARRIORS (NISQUALLY + YAKIMA) LED BY OWHI + LESCHI, ATTACKED SEATTLE...

THEY WERE BETRAYED BY INFORMANTS + RETREATED UNDER FIRE FROM US MARINES. 200 SALISH MAY HAVE DIED.

IN 1858, 2 US SHIPS WERE ATTACKED + DESTROYED AT HAIDA GWAII, WITH ANOTHER THE NEXT YEAR BY THE NUU-CHAH-NULTH...

IN 1860, A GUNBOAT WAS SENT TO QUADRA ISLAND TO PACIFY THE LEKWILTOK~KWAKIUTL. CANNON FIRE DESTROYED THE PEOPLE'S HOUSES...

IN 1862, A SMALLPOX EPIDEMIC BEGAN IN VICTORIA. COLONIAL AUTHORITIES FORCED HUNDREDS OF NATIVES OUT.

INFECTED, THEY RETURNED TO THEIR VILLAGES, SPREADING THE DISEASE. AN ESTIMATED 1 IN 3 DIED IN 2 YEARS. THE EPIDEMIC OCCURRED AS MORE EUROPEAN SETTLERS ARRIVED.

IN 1863, 2 SETTLERS WERE KILLED ON SALTSPRING ISLAND. A LARGE NAVAL FORCE OF 4 SHIPS WAS SENT AGAINST THE LEMALCHI (PART OF THE COWICHAN).

THE LEMALCHI RESISTED. AFTER THEIR VILLAGE WAS BOMBED THEY EVADED MARINES FOR A MONTH. SEVERAL WARRIORS WERE CAUGHT + EXECUTED.

IN SEPTEMBER 1863, A GUNBOAT WAS SENT TO PORT SIMPSON AFTER SETTLERS WERE KILLED.

TSIMSHIAN VILLAGES WERE RAIDED AND SEVERAL CHIEFS TAKEN PRISONER. THE SUSPECTS WERE SURRENDERED.

IN 1864, ANOTHER SHIP WAS ATTACKED + ITS CREW KILLED BY NUU-CHAH-NULTH.

BOOM!

GUNBOATS WERE SENT AGAINST THE AHOUSAT, PART OF THE NUU-CHAH-NULTH. 9 AHOUSAT VILLAGES WERE DESTROYED + AT LEAST 15 KILLED...

IN 1865, A CUSTOMS OFFICIAL WAS KILLED BY NUXALK WARRIORS AT BELLA COOLA.

IN DECEMBER 1865, A KWAKIUTL VILLAGE NEAR FT. RUPERT WAS RAIDED BY A GUNBOAT. THE KWAKIUTL RESISTED + THEIR HOUSES + CANOES WERE BOMBED.

IN EARLY 1868, OWIKEENO WARRIORS ATTACKED + DESTROYED A TRADE SHIP.

IN JUNE 1868, KWAKIUTL ATTACKED A SHIP BUT WERE REPELLED BY A NEW REPEATING RIFLE. 15 WERE KILLED...

IN 1869, 2 YEARS AFTER PURCHASING ALASKA FROM THE RUSSIANS, US SHIPS BOMBED TLINGIT VILLAGES AT KAKE + WRANGELL...

IN ONE ATTACK, 29 HOUSES WERE DESTROYED.

IN MAY 1869, A VESSEL WAS SHIPWRECKED. THERE WERE NO *SURVIVORS*, ALTHOUGH HEADLESS CORPSES WERE LATER FOUND.

THE HESQUIAT WERE SUSPECTED, AND SEVERAL WARRIORS TAKEN PRISONER. 2 WERE HUNG IN FRONT OF THE VILLAGE.

IN 1873, OWIKEENO WARRIORS ATTACKED + DESTROYED THE GEORGE S. WRIGHT NEAR RIVER'S INLET (IT WAS SHIPWRECKED).

IN 1877, A GUNBOAT WENT TO RIVER'S INLET + TOOK 2 PRISONERS. 2 NUXALK WERE IDENTIFIED AS TAKING PART...

BOOM!!

AT KIMSQUIT, THE NUXALK REFUSED TO SURRENDER THE SUSPECTS + THEIR VILLAGE WAS DESTROYED BY CANNON...

THE KIMSQUIT BOMBING WAS THE LAST USE OF ROYAL NAVY FIREPOWER ON THE COAST OF 'BRITISH COLUMBIA'.

IN 1882, THE TLINGIT VILLAGE OF ANGOON WAS DESTROYED BY US NAVAL BOMBARDMENT AFTER A SETTLER WAS KILLED.

BY 1881, THERE WERE SOME 23,000 SETTLERS IN 'BC', + 25,000 NATIVES (FROM A POPULATION OF 200,000 IN 1780).

MISSION ASSIMILATION

HOLY BIBLE

DUE TO DISEASE, DIVISION, + COLONIAL FIREPOWER, COAST TRIBES WERE UNABLE TO RESIST. THEY WERE FORCED ONTO RESERVES + SUBJECTED TO ASSIMILATION.

NO JUSTICE ON STOLEN LAND

BRITISH COLUMBIA IS UNIQUE IN CANADA IN THAT ALMOST NO TREATIES WERE MADE DURING ITS COLONIZATION...

The 'Douglas Treaties'
Vancouver Island

Fort Rupert
(2 in 1851)
Nanaimo (1 in 1854)
Saanich (2 in 1851)
Victoria (9 in 1850)

Total: 358 sq. km

FROM 1850-54, 14 TREATIES WERE MADE ON VANCOUVER ISLAND FOR SMALL PIECES OF LAND (THE 'DOUGLAS TREATIES').

IN 1899, A PORTION OF NORTH-EAST BC WAS INCLUDED AS PART OF TREATY NO. 8. OTHERWISE, 'BC' IS UNCEDED TERRITORY.

Treaty No. 11 1921
Treaty 8 1899
Treaty 10 1906
Treaty 5 1875
Treaty 6 1876, 1889
7 1877
Treaty 4 1879

BY THEIR OWN LAWS, THE BRITISH WERE LEGALLY BOUND TO MAKE TREATIES WITH NATIVES IN EXCHANGE FOR LAND...

THESE LAWS INCLUDED THE 1763 ROYAL PROCLAMATION. FOR THIS REASON, BRITAIN (+ LATER CANADA) MADE TREATIES IN EXCHANGE FOR LARGE TRACTS OF LAND.

THESE INCL. THE NUMBERED TREATIES MADE DURING CANADA'S WESTWARD EXPANSION ACROSS THE PRAIRIES. CITING LACK OF FUNDS, THIS WASN'T DONE IN BC.

IN 1871, BC BECAME A PART OF CANADA. IN 1874, THE BC LANDS ACT WAS PASSED TO OPEN LAND TO SETTLEMENT.

1874 BC LANDS ACT

1875 DUTY OF DISALLOWANCE

CANADA ISSUED THE 1875 DUTY-OF-DISALLOWANCE, STRIKING DOWN THE BC LANDS ACT + CITING THE FAILURE OF THE PROVINCE TO MAKE TREATIES LEGALLY SURRENDERING NATIVE LAND.

IN RESPONSE, BC THREATENED TO WITHDRAW FROM CANADA...

1876 INDIAN ACT

BAND COUNCILS
RESERVES
STATUS

IN 1876, CANADA ISSUED THE INDIAN ACT, EXTENDING GOVERNMENT CONTROL OVER ALL NATIVES, INC. THOSE IN 'BC', 'LEGALIZING' THE THEFT OF NATIVE LAND!

PART 3: ASSIMILATION

A COMMON STRATEGY OF COLONIAL REGIMES IS TO ASSIMILATE SURVIVING NATIVE PEOPLES INTO THE COLONIAL SOCIETY ITSELF...

THIS MAKES THE NATIVE EASIER TO CONTROL AS WELL AS AN OBEDIENT WORKER AND CONSUMER IN THE COLONIAL SYSTEM...

IN THE AMERICAS, THIS WAS DONE BY FORCING NATIVE CHILDREN TO ATTEND SCHOOLS RUN BY CHURCHES + PRIESTS.

THEY WERE KNOWN AS MISSIONS, INDUSTRIAL, OR RESIDENTIAL SCHOOLS...

BEFORE

AFTER

CHILDREN WERE FORBIDDEN TO SPEAK THEIR LANGUAGE OR PRACTISE THEIR CULTURE. MANY WERE ABUSED BY PRIESTS + STAFF.

RELIGION AND SCHOOLS ARE THE MAIN FORMS OF ASSIMILATING NATIVE PEOPLES.

THRU THESE, THE NATIVE'S CULTURE AND HISTORY ARE ERASED, REPLACED BY THOSE OF THE OCCUPYING NATION...

IN N. AMERICA, RESIDENTIAL SCHOOLS EXISTED FROM THE MID-1800s UNTIL THE 1980s.

ENTIRE GENERATIONS WERE FORCED TO ADAPT EUROPEAN CULTURE + VALUES. TODAY'S GENERATIONS ARE THE MOST ASSIMILATED AND COLONIZED...

A GOOD EXAMPLE OF ASSIMILATION IS THE ROMAN COLONIZATION OF WESTERN EUROPE. SOME REGIONS WERE OCCUPIED FOR AS LONG AS 500 YEARS...

ALTHO' THE EUROPEAN TRIBES RESISTED, OVER TIME MOST HAD BECOME 'LATINIZED', WITH MANY LATER SERVING IN THE ROMAN ARMY OR GOVERNMENT...

IN N. AMERICA, RESERVATIONS WERE IMPORTANT TO REMOVE THE PEOPLE FROM THEIR LAND AND IMPOSE EUROPEAN CULTURE.

BEFORE

AFTER

SHELTER IS ONE EXAMPLE: INSTEAD OF MANY SHARING ONE SHELTER, NATIVES WERE FORCED TO LIVE IN EUROPEAN-STYLE HOUSES.

THRU LOSS OF CULTURE + DESTRUCTION OF TERRITORY, INDIGENOUS PEOPLES HAVE BECOME DEPENDENT ON STATE FUNDING...

BEFORE

AFTER

THIS MAKES THEM MORE EASILY CONTROLLED AND VULNERABLE TO BOTH GOVERNMENT AND CORPORATE PRESSURE FOR RESOURCES.

TODAY, ENGLISH, FRENCH, SPANISH, GERMAN + ITALIAN HAVE THEIR ROOTS IN LATIN, THE RESULT OF ROMAN INVASION + CONQUEST...

WESTERN CIVILIZATION IS ITSELF THE RESULT OF ASSIMILATING EUROPEAN TRIBAL NATIONS INTO THE ROMAN EMPIRE...

THRU LAWS SUCH AS THE INDIAN ACT, TRADITIONAL FORMS OF GOVERNMENT AND ORGANIZATION WERE BANNED...

BEFORE

AFTER

IN PLACE OF THESE, BAND COUNCILS WERE IMPOSED, BASED ON EUROPEAN MODELS OF GOVERNMENT AND SOCIAL CONTROL...

TO THIS END, STATES CONTINUE POLICIES OF LEGAL, POLITICAL + ECONOMIC ASSIMILATION OF NATIVE PEOPLES + RESERVE LAND...

THEIR GOAL IS TO DESTROY ALL INDIGENOUS CULTURE + IDENTITY THAT INSPIRES OUR SPIRIT OF RESISTANCE, AND WHICH LIMITS THEIR PLANS OF EXPLOITATION...

'68 REBELLION

IN THE 1960 s, THERE WAS WORLD-WIDE REBELLION AS OPPRESSED PEOPLES ORGANIZED THEMSELVES TO FIGHT THE IMPERIAL SYSTEM. MANY COUNTRIES SAW RIOTS, OCCUPATIONS, + ARMED RESISTANCE (INCL. CANADA + THE USA).

THIS GLOBAL UPRISING WAS INSPIRED BY THE *FIERCE* RESISTANCE OF THE VIETNAMESE PEOPLE FIGHTING **US** INVASION + OCCUPATION (1963-75)...

INSIDE THE **US**, MILITANT BLACK RESISTANCE HAD INCREASED SINCE THE 1950 s CIVIL RIGHTS STRUGGLE...

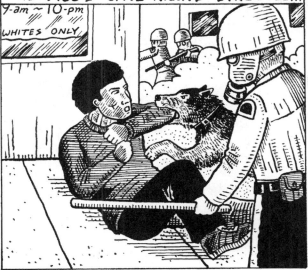

ALTHO' *PACIFISTS* LIKE MARTIN LUTHER KING WERE PROMOTED BY THE STATE, MANY BLACKS SAW THE *LOGIC* IN MALCOLM X'S IDEAS ON SELF-DEFENSE.

IN OAKLAND, CALIFORNIA, THE BLACK PANTHER PARTY FOR SELF-DEFENSE WAS FORMED IN THE EARLY 1960s.

THE PANTHERS SOON HAD CHAPTERS ACROSS THE US; THEY ORGANIZED PROTESTS, EDUCATION CLASSES, AND BREAKFAST PROGRAMS FOR CHILDREN.

MANY OTHER MOVEMENTS AROSE AT THIS TIME IN THE US, SUCH AS STUDENTS, WOMEN, GAYS, CHICANOS, + A STRONG ANTI-WAR MOVEMENT...

1968 WAS THE PEAK OF THE GLOBAL REBELLION. IN VIETNAM, GUERRILLAS LAUNCHED THE 'TET OFFENSIVE'...

DESPITE 500,000 TROOPS IN S. VIETNAM, THE US COULDN'T STOP THE INSURGENCY.

IN ASIA, AFRICA, + SOUTH AMERICA, STUDENTS + WORKERS CARRIED OUT MASSIVE PROTESTS, STRIKES, + RIOTS.

IN MAY, A GENERAL STRIKE + DAYS OF MASS RIOTS THREATENED TO OVERTHROW THE GOVERNMENT IN FRANCE.

ACROSS THE US, NATIONAL GUARD TROOPS WERE DEPLOYED TO CRUSH RIOTS BY MOSTLY URBAN BLACKS; SCORES WERE KILLED.

1968 WAS ALSO THE YEAR THAT THE AMERICAN INDIAN MOVEMENT WAS FORMED, IN MINNEAPOLIS...

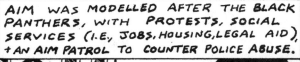

AIM WAS MODELLED AFTER THE BLACK PANTHERS, WITH PROTESTS, SOCIAL SERVICES (I.E., JOBS, HOUSING, LEGAL AID), + AN AIM PATROL TO COUNTER POLICE ABUSE.

THE AMERICAN INDIAN MOVEMENT

AIM WAS PART OF A RENEWED INDIGENOUS STRUGGLE IN N. AMERICA THAT BEGAN IN THE EARLY 1960s...

ON THE NORTHWEST COAST, THE PEOPLE BEGAN TO FISH WITHOUT PERMITS. MANY WERE ARRESTED, INCLUDING ELDERS.

AS MORE NATIVES ENTERED COLLEGE, THEY ALSO BEGAN TO ORGANIZE...

WE SHOULD HAVE NATIVE STUDIES~ AT SCHOOL!

WOW!

BY 1968, A NETWORK OF NATIVE 'GRASSROOTS' GROUPS EXISTED, IN CONTRAST TO THE STATE-FUNDED NATIONAL CONGRESS OF AMERICAN INDIANS.

ZZZZ

INDIANS DON'T DEMONSTRATE!

NATIONAL CONGRESS OF AMERICAN INDIANS

BIA

THE NCAI'S VIEWS WERE EXPRESSED IN A BANNER AT ITS 1967 CONVENTION: "INDIANS DON'T DEMONSTRATE"...

AIM WAS PART OF A NEW GENERATION, INSPIRED BY THE 1960s REVOLTS; AS URBANIZED NATIVES, THEY WERE ALSO EXPOSED TO NEW MOVEMENTS + IDEAS.

KILL THE RICH

AS A RESULT, THEY WERE AWARE OF THEIR OPPRESSION AND MORE DETERMINED TO MAKE CHANGE...

WHILE AIM WAS STARTING UP, AN OCCUPATION BEGAN OF **ALCATRAZ** ISLAND, IN SAN FRANCISCO BAY...

ALCATRAZ WAS A FORMER HIGH SECURITY PRISON. LEFT ABANDONED, ALCATRAZ WOULD BE OCCUPIED FROM NOVEMBER 1969 TO JUNE 1971 (19 MONTHS).

ALCATRAZ WAS THE FIRST ACTION BY INDIGENOUS PEOPLE IN THE **US** TO GET NATIONAL MEDIA COVERAGE...

THOUSANDS OF NATIVE PEOPLE WENT TO ALCATRAZ. FOR MANY, IT WAS THEIR FIRST TIME PARTICIPATING IN INDIGENOUS CULTURE + CEREMONIES.

ALCATRAZ *INSPIRED* NATIVE PEOPLE ACROSS THE COUNTRY, WITH MANY **OCCUPATIONS** OF GOVERNMENT PROPERTY DURING AND AFTER...

AS MORE NATIVE PEOPLE BECAME **ACTIVE**, AIM CONTINUED TO WORK IN THE MID-WEST. NOT UNTIL 1972 DID AIM REALLY GROW, HOWEVER...

IN FEBRUARY 1972, RAY YELLOW THUNDER WAS BEATEN + KILLED BY 4 WHITES IN GORDON, NEBRASKA. HIS FAMILY AT PINE RIDGE DEMANDED **JUSTICE.**

LOCAL AUTHORITIES DID NOTHING. THE FAMILY ASKED THE TRIBAL COUNCIL FOR HELP. FINALLY, THEY TURNED TO AIM...

AIM ORGANIZED 3 DAYS OF PROTESTS, PUBLIC MEETINGS AND BOYCOTTS IN GORDON; MOST WHITES IN TOWN FLED...

OVER 1,000 NATIVES TOOK PART; AS A RESULT, 4 WHITES WERE CHARGED WITH MANSLAUGHTER + 1 COP WAS SUSPENDED.

THIS WAS A GREAT VICTORY FOR AIM, ONE THAT SAW BOTH RESERVATION AND URBAN NATIVES JOINING TOGETHER...

IN OCTOBER 1972, AIM TOOK PART IN THE TRAIL OF BROKEN TREATIES, A CARAVAN STARTING ON THE WEST COAST.

THE CARAVAN STOPPED AT CITIES AND RESERVES ON ITS WAY TO WASHINGTON, D.C., RAISING AWARENESS OF NATIVE TREATY RIGHTS + SOCIAL CONDITIONS...

WHEN THE CARAVAN ARRIVED IN WASHINGTON, OFFICIALS REFUSED TO MEET OR DISCUSS THEIR DEMANDS.

ON NOVEMBER 2, SEVERAL HUNDRED NATIVES OCCUPIED THE BUREAU OF INDIAN AFFAIRS HEADQUARTERS. THEY FOUGHT WITH RIOT COPS + PREPARED FOR A FINAL ASSAULT...

THE OCCUPATION LASTED 6 DAYS. THE BIA OFFICES WERE BADLY DAMAGED, AND WHEN THEY LEFT, AIM MEMBERS TOOK OVER 20,000 POUNDS OF FILES...

BY NOW, MANY NATIVE VETERANS OF THE VIETNAM WAR HAD JOINED, ADDING TO THE MILITANCY OF THE MOVEMENT.

IN JANUARY 1973, ANOTHER LAKOTA WAS KILLED BY A WHITE SETTLER IN SOUTH DAKOTA...

WESLEY BAD HEART BULL WAS STABBED TO DEATH. HIS KILLER WAS CHARGED WITH 2ND DEGREE MANSLAUGHTER + RELEASED.

ON FEBRUARY 6 '73, AIM AND MANY LAKOTAS WENT TO CUSTER, S. DAKOTA, FOR THE ACCUSED'S COURT HEARING.

THEY DEMANDED MURDER CHARGES BE LAID. WHEN THEY TRIED TO ENTER THE COURT, RIOT COPS STOPPED THEM.

A RIOT ERUPTED, WITH SEVERAL BUILDINGS AND POLICE CARS SET ON FIRE. COPS FACED OFF WITH ARMED AIM MEMBERS; 30 PEOPLE WERE ARRESTED.

WOUNDED KNEE '73

BY 1973, AIM HAD STRONG CONNECTIONS TO TRADITIONAL LAKOTAS ON THE PINE RIDGE RESERVATION IN SOUTH DAKOTA.

THE TRIBAL PRESIDENT- DICK WILSON - WAS CORRUPT + VIOLENTLY OPPOSED TO AIM + TRADITIONALISTS ON THE REZ...

AIM? YOU MEAN THOSE ASSHOLES IN MOCASSINS?

WITH GOVERNMENT HELP, WILSON SET UP A PARAMILITARY GROUP KNOWN AS THE GOONs (GUARDIANS OF THE OGLALA NATION)...

THE GOONS TERRORIZED THE REZ AND ALL OPPOSITION TO WILSON, CREATING A CLIMATE OF FEAR + INSECURITY...

AFTER THE CUSTER RIOT, 65 US MARSHALLS WERE SENT TO PINE RIDGE, ALONG WITH MORE FBI + BIA POLICE, TO BACK WILSON...

WITH MANY PEOPLE ORGANIZING TO REMOVE HIM FROM OFFICE, WILSON BANNED ALL PUBLIC MEETINGS + GATHERINGS...

AFTER A SECRET MEETING ON FEBRUARY 27, THE PEOPLE DECIDED TO TAKE ACTION: THEY WOULD OCCUPY WOUNDED KNEE, SITE OF THE 1890 MASSACRE. OVER 200 TRAVELLED BY CAR THAT NIGHT.

THAT SAME NIGHT, GOONS + BIA POLICE SET UP ROAD-BLOCKS INTO WOUNDED KNEE. THE SIEGE HAD BEGUN...

ON FEB. 28, MILITARY ADVISORS ALONG WITH TWO ARMOURED PERSONNEL CARRIERS WERE SENT TO WOUNDED KNEE...

ALTOGETHER, 17 APCS, HELICOPTERS, JETS, AMMUNITION, FLARES + GRENADES WOULD BE SUPPLIED BY THE MILITARY...

DURING THE SIEGE, TENS OF THOUSANDS OF ROUNDS WOULD BE FIRED BY FBI, POLICE, MARSHALLS + GOONS INTO WOUNDED KNEE.

2 AIM MEMBERS ~ BUDDY LAMONT + FRANK CLEARWATER ~ WERE SHOT + KILLED. SEVERAL POLICE WERE INJURED AS WELL...

ON MAY 9, THE DEFENDERS LAID DOWN THEIR ARMS + SURRENDERED. ALTOGETHER, 562 PEOPLE WOULD BE ARRESTED, ALTHO' AFTER 3 YEARS OF TRIALS, ONLY 15 WERE CONVICTED.

THE 71-DAY SIEGE AT WOUNDED KNEE SERVED TO RE-AWAKEN OUR INDIGENOUS WARRIOR SPIRIT AND STRENGTHEN OUR WILL TO RESIST.

WHILE NEGOTIATIONS DRAGGED ON, FOOD, AMMO, + MEDICAL SUPPLIES HAD TO BE SMUGGLED IN PAST THE PERIMETER...

THE 'OKA CRISIS'

DURING THE SUMMER OF 1990, A 77-DAY ARMED STANDOFF OCCURRED IN THE MOHAWK TERRITORIES OF **KAHNAWAKE** AND **KANEHSATAKE/OKA**, NEAR MONTREAL.

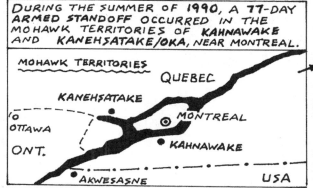

MOHAWK TERRITORIES

QUEBEC

KANEHSATAKE

TO OTTAWA

ONT.

MONTREAL

KAHNAWAKE

AKWESASNE

USA

MOHAWK WARRIORS CONFRONTED OVER 2,000 QUEBEC POLICE AND 4,500 CANADIAN SOLDIERS...

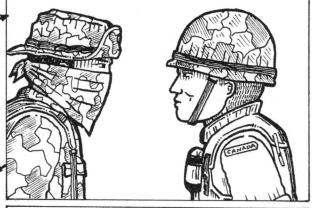

IN KANEHSATAKE, THE TOWN OF OKA HAD PLANNED TO EXPAND A GOLF COURSE INTO 'THE PINES', A SMALL FORESTED AREA CONTAINING A MOHAWK GRAVEYARD.

STOP PLAYING GOLF!

NO MORE GOLF COURSES

SAVE THE PINES

IN 1989, MOHAWKS AND RESIDENTS OF OKA BEGAN PROTESTS + PETITIONS TO STOP IT...

IN THE SPRING OF 1990, MOHAWKS SET UP A CAMP IN THE PINES AND BLOCKED A SMALL, DIRT ROAD...

ON JULY 11, 1990, OVER 100 HEAVILY-ARMED QUEBEC POLICE ATTACKED THE MOHAWK BLOCKADE, SHOOTING TEAR GAS + AUTOMATIC WEAPONS. MOHAWK WARRIORS RETURNED FIRE; IN A BRIEF FIRE FIGHT, ONE POLICE MAN WAS **SHOT + KILLED**...

MOHAWK TERRITORY

NO TRESPASSING

THE POLICE FLED, ABANDONING MANY VEHICLES. THESE WERE USED TO BUILD NEW BARRICADES...

GET BACK! BACK UP!

AT NEARBY KAHNAWAKE, WARRIORS SIEZED THE MERCIER BRIDGE, A VITAL COMMUTER LINK TO MONTREAL...

HUNDREDS OF POLICE ARRIVED + SEALED OFF THE AREA; ADVISORS + EQUIPMENT FROM THE MILITARY WERE ALSO SENT...

MOHAWK? DO YOU LIVE IN OKA?

IN KANEHSATAKE, WARRIORS FORTIFIED THEIR POSITIONS; REINFORCEMENTS AND SUPPLIES WERE SMUGGLED IN...

AT KAHNAWAKE (POP. 7,000), ENTRANCES WERE BARRICADED. FOOD, MEDICAL AID, AND COMMUNICATIONS WERE ORGANIZED.

SEE YOU AT THE MEETING!

AS THE SIEGE WENT ON, WHITE MOBS FROM NEARBY TOWNS BEGAN TO RIOT. THEY DEMANDED POLICE RE-OPEN THE BRIDGE.

ON AUGUST 20, THE CANADIAN ARMED FORCES TOOK OVER FROM POLICE AT BOTH KAHNAWAKE + KANEHSATAKE.

4,500 TROOPS WOULD BE DEPLOYED, WITH LEOPARD TANKS, APCS, HELICOPTERS, FIGHTER JETS, ARTILLERY, AND NAVAL VESSELS IN THE ST. LAWRENCE RIVER.

IN KAHNAWAKE, SOME MOHAWKS WANTED OUT. ON AUG. 28, AFTER BEING DELAYED BY POLICE, A CONVOY WAS ATTACKED BY WHITE MOBS; THE POLICE DID NOTHING...

AT KANEHSATAKE, WARRIORS RETREATED AS THE ARMY ADVANCED, ENDING UP IN A TREATMENT CENTER BY SEPTEMBER...

ON SEPTEMBER 18, SOLDIERS RAIDED TEKAKWITHA ISLAND (OFF OF KAHNAWAKE). THEY SHOT TEAR GAS + LIVE AMMO AS MOHAWKS RESISTED...

THE SOLDIERS WERE LATER EVACUATED BY HELICOPTERS...

ACROSS THE COUNTRY, NATIVE PEOPLE SHOWED THEIR **SOLIDARITY** WITH THE MOHAWKS THRU PROTESTS, OCCUPATIONS, ROAD + RAIL BLOCKADES, + SABOTAGE...

CANADA FACED AN INDIGENOUS UPRISING IF IT USED **FORCE** TO END THE SIEGE.

IN BC + ALBERTA, RAIL WAY BRIDGES WERE DESTROYED BY FIRE...

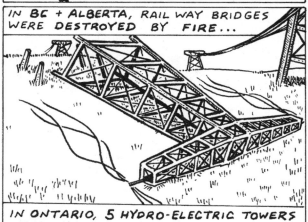

IN ONTARIO, 5 HYDRO-ELECTRIC TOWERS WERE CUT DOWN BY SABOTEURS...

OKA SERVED TO REVITALIZE THE **WARRIOR SPIRIT** OF INDIGENOUS PEOPLES AND OUR **WILL TO RESIST**...

ALTHO' THE GOVERNMENT AND MEDIA PORTRAYED THE WARRIORS AS CRIMINALS + TERRORISTS, MANY SAW THEM AS HEROES DEFENDING THEIR PEOPLE...

ON SEPT. 26, THE LAST HOLD OUTS AT KANEHSATAKE BURNED THEIR WEAPONS AND WALKED OUT...

MOST WERE LATER FOUND **NOT GUILTY** OF WEAPONS + RIOT CHARGES. THE OKA GOLF COURSE WAS NEVER EXPANDED...

ZAPATISTAS

ON JANUARY 1ST, 1994, THE ZAPATISTA ARMY OF NATIONAL LIBERATION (EZLN) LAUNCHED ITS OFFENSIVE IN THE SOUTHERN MEXICAN STATE OF CHIAPAS.

THEY CAPTURED 5 TOWNS, INCLUDING SAN CRISTOBAL + OCOSINGO (POP. 100,000).

THEY TOOK OVER RADIO STATIONS TO BROADCAST MESSAGES TO THE PEOPLE.

THIS IS A DECLARATION OF WAR FROM THE ZAPATISTA ARMY OF NATIONAL LIBERATION...

THEIR DEMANDS INCLUDED REJECTION OF NAFTA* (IMPLEMENTED JAN. 1/94) AS WELL AS LAND + FREEDOM...
*(N. AMERICAN FREE TRADE AGREEMENT).

ZAPATISTA FIGHTERS TOOK CONTROL OF GOVERNMENT BUILDINGS AND FOUGHT GUN BATTLES WITH POLICE + SOLDIERS.

THE MEXICAN ARMY COUNTER-ATTACKED, DEPLOYING SEVERAL THOUSAND TROOPS WITH APC's, ARTILLERY, FIGHTER JETS + HELICOPTERS. AS MANY AS 400 CIVILIANS MAY HAVE BEEN KILLED.

THE HEAVIEST FIGHTING WAS IN OCOSINGO, WHERE OVER 50 EZLN WARRIORS MAY HAVE BEEN KILLED...

SOME WERE FOUND WITH THEIR HANDS TIED BEHIND THEIR BACKS-THEY WERE EXECUTED BY SOLDIERS.

BY JANUARY 4, ZAPATISTA UNITS HAD ALL WITHDRAWN TO THEIR BASES IN THE LACANDON JUNGLE.

BY JANUARY 12, 14,000 MEXICAN TROOPS HAD BEEN DEPLOYED. THEY RAIDED TOWNS + VILLAGES, WITH HOUSE-TO-HOUSE SEARCHES + MASS ARRESTS.

ZAPATISTA WOMEN WARRIORS

BUT THE ZAPATISTAS ESCAPED. COMPRISED OF MAYAN INDIANS, THE EZLN HAD TRAINED AND ORGANIZED IN SECRET FOR 10 YEARS...

THEY TOOK THEIR NAME FROM AN INDIGENOUS LEADER IN THE 1910 REVOLUTION: EMILIANO ZAPATA.

BY SPRING, HUNDREDS OF OCCUPATIONS + LAND SEIZURES HAD OCCURED. MANY NATIVES WERE INSPIRED TO REBEL...

ALL ACROSS MEXICO, WORKERS, STUDENTS, THE POOR, + OTHER SOCIAL MOVEMENTS RALLIED IN SUPPORT OF THE INSURGENTS.

MANY TOWNS IN CHIAPAS DECLARED THEMSELVES AUTONOMOUS FROM THE STATE + ALLIED WITH THE ZAPATISTAS.

THEY SELF-ORGANIZED SCHOOLS, LOCAL GOVERNMENT, HEALTH CLINICS, AND WORKER'S CO-OPS TO SELL FOOD AND CRAFTS (INCLUDING CORN + COFFEE).

THE ZAPATISTAS HAVE ALSO ORGANIZED INTERNATIONAL GATHERINGS WITH DELEGATES FROM AROUND THE WORLD.

NATIONAL MOBILIZATIONS UNDER THE EZLN BANNER HAVE INVOLVED TENS OF THOUSANDS - FOCUSING ON LAND AND THE RIGHTS OF INDIGENOUS PEOPLE.

AS PART OF MEXICO'S COUNTER-INSURGENCY WAR, MASSACRES, ASSASSINATIONS, TORTURE + IMPRISONMENT ARE USED.

IN 1997, 47 PEASANTS WERE MASSACRED BY RANCH-HANDS ORGANIZED INTO A PARAMILITARY FORCE IN ACTEAL...

I'M AN INSURGENT. I HAVE DEDICATED ALL MY LIFE AND TIME TO THE CAUSE.*

* MAJOR ANNA MARIA, EZLN

DESPITE THIS, THE EZLN CONTINUES TO EXIST, ORGANIZE + MOBILIZE AMONG MEXICO'S INDIGENOUS PEOPLES...

TODAY, THE ZAPATISTA SPIRIT OF INSURGENCY HAS SPREAD THRU MEXICO AND THE WORLD. IN 2006, THE EZLN LAUNCHED THE 'OTHER CAMPAIGN' TO UNIFY SOCIAL MOVEMENTS. THAT YEAR, REVOLTS AT ATENCO & OAXACA SHOOK THE COUNTRY, AS DID PRESIDENTIAL ELECTIONS MARKED BY FRAUD...

1995 STANDOFF AT TS'PETEN

IN 1995, A MONTH-LONG STANDOFF OCCURED IN 'BRITISH COLUMBIA' BETWEEN NATIVES AND POLICE. IN A FIRE FIGHT ON SEPT. 11, POLICE FIRED TENS OF 1,000s OF ROUNDS + BLEW UP A TRUCK. ALTHO' LIGHTLY ARMED, THE WARRIORS SUCCEEDED IN DISABLING A 'BISON' ARMOURED PERSONNEL CARRIER USED BY POLICE.

IN 1989, A SUNDANCE CAMP WAS SET UP AT TS'PETEN *

* CHA-PA-TEN (BIG LAKE), KNOWN AS GUSTAFSEN LAKE (IN SECWEPMEC TERRITORY)

IN 1995, A LOCAL RANCHER ASKED THE POLICE TO EVICT THE CAMP. IN JUNE AND JULY, RANCH HANDS BEGAN TO HARASS + THREATEN AN ELDER + HIS FAMILY LIVING IN THE CAMP. THE ELDER CALLED FOR HELP, AND WARRIORS CAME TO DEFEND THEM AND ASSERT NATIVE SOVEREIGNTY.

"BC" 'ALBERTA'

TS'PETEN (Gustafsen L.)

VANCOUVER

'USA'

LIKE MOST OF BC, SECWEPMEC TERRITORY REMAINS UNCEDED, FOR WHICH NO TREATIES WERE EVER MADE ~ A VIOLATION OF BRITISH, CANADIAN + INTERNATIONAL LAW...

THIS SOVEREIGNTY WAS THE POSITION OF THE DEFENDERS, WHO DEMANDED CANADA ABIDE BY ITS OWN LAWS + END THE ILLEGAL OCCUPATION OF 'BC'.

SO UNDER THESE LAWS, CANADA AND THE ROYAL CANADIAN MOUNTED POLICE HAVE NO JURISDICTION!

THE DEFENDERS REFUSED TO MOVE. ON AUG. 18, THEY FOUND A HEAVILY-ARMED EMERGENCY RESPONSE TEAM (ERT) DOING SURVEILLANCE ON THEM.

HEY! WHO THE...?!

S@*T!

AT THE SAME TIME, POLICE BEGAN AERIAL SURVEILLANCE ~ HIGH FLYING PLANES WITH POWERFUL CAMERAS...

THEY ALSO ASKED THE CANADIAN ARMY FOR HELP.

CRAZY COPS!

RCMP HELP! ARMED INDIANS

THE RCMP EVEN REQUESTED 'HELP' IN THE FORM OF BISON APCS, 8-WHEELED, 14 TON VEHICLES...

POLICE

GRRRRRRR

ON AUGUST 21, FOUR BISONS WERE MOVED TO AN ARMOURY IN KAMLOOPS (150 KM SOUTH).

ON AUGUST 24, DEFENDERS FIRED SHOTS AT A POLICE HELICOPTER (IT WAS REALLY ANNOYING!).

BAM! BAM! BAM!

BAM!

AT THIS TIME, POLICE SEALED OFF THE AREA WITH CHECKPOINTS ON ROADS...

THEY ALSO CUT THE CAMP'S RADIO-PHONE, MAKING IT A DIRECT LINE TO POLICE ONLY.

AS A RESULT, THE DEFENDERS COULDN'T COMMUNICATE TO THE PUBLIC...

THESE PEOPLE ARE TERRORISTS...

GOD-DAMN THOSE INDIANS!

THE MEDIA REPORTED ONLY THE POLICE AND GOVERNMENT VERSION OF EVENTS.

THE RCMP USED THE MEDIA TO SPREAD LIES AND DISINFORMATION...

SMEAR CAMPAIGNS ARE OUR SPECIALTY!*

*ACTUAL QUOTE: SERGEANT MONTAGUE IN RCMP VIDEO DOCUMENTATION OF THE SIEGE - EXPOSED DURING TRIAL IN '97.

ON AUGUST 27, POLICE CLAIMED A SUBURBAN USED BY THEIR ERT HAD BEEN AMBUSHED. FLAK VESTS SAVED THE COP'S LIVES...

NO ONE WAS CHARGED IN RELATION TO THIS, NOR WAS THERE ANY CAMERA FOOTAGE. DEFENDERS CLAIM POLICE FABRICATED THE ENTIRE 'AMBUSH'.

AROUND THIS TIME, A SECRET RCMP AND MILITARY COMMAND POST WAS SET UP: 'CAMP ZULU'.

ZULU HAD A FIELD HOSPITAL, KITCHEN, COMMUNICATIONS, AND SLEEPING QUARTERS...

ON SEPTEMBER 4, POLICE REPORTED A SECOND 'ATTACK' ON A SUBURBAN...

THWAK

DURING THE TRIAL, WHAT POLICE SAID WAS A BULLET STRIKE TURNED OUT TO BE A TREE BRANCH HITTING THE TRUCK...

THE NEXT DAY, POLICE PUBLICLY DEPLOYED ALL THE BISONS, CITING THE PREVIOUS DAY'S 'ATTACK' ON THEIR OFFICERS...

GRRRRR

INSIDE THE CAMP, THE DEFENDERS HELD DAILY MEETINGS. THEY PRAYED AND SMUDGED FOR SPIRITUAL PROTECTION...

THEY ALSO MAINTAINED THEIR ARMED DEFENSE WITH TRENCHES + PATROLS...

ON SEPT. 10, A DELEGATION OF SECWEPMEC ELDERS VISITED THE CAMP; A NO-SHOOT ZONE WAS SET UP WITH POLICE, AND NEGOTIATIONS WERE ONGOING...

BOOOM

ON SEPT. 11, HOWEVER, POLICE AMBUSHED A TRUCK USED BY THE DEFENDERS IN A NO-SHOOT ZONE. AS THE TRUCK DROVE DOWN A ROAD, EXPLOSIVES HIDDEN IN THE GROUND WERE DETONATED...

THE TWO OCCUPANTS FLED THE DISABLED TRUCK ~ UNARMED ~ ALONG WITH A DOG...

LET'S GO!

GRRRR

SMASH!

THEN A BISON APC HIDDEN IN THE FOREST DROVE OUT + RAMMED THE TRUCK.

POLICE ON FOOT OPENED FIRE, KILLING THE DOG...

BAM! BAM!

AS THE TWO DEFENDERS SWAM ACROSS A LAKE, POLICE IN THE APC OPENED FIRE.

BAM!

AT THIS TIME, OTHER DEFENDERS OPENED FIRE ON THE APC, WHICH BEGAN TO PURSUE THE SHOOTERS...

BAM!

GRRRR

SMASHING THRU THE FOREST, THE BISON BECAME DISABLED WHEN ONE OF ITS WHEEL AXLES WAS BROKEN...

BAM! BAM!

BAM! BAM!

SMASH

GRRRR

THIS WAS THE RESULT OF THE APC HITTING A TREE, ALONG WITH RIFLE FIRE BY SECWEPMEC ELDER WOLVERINE...

INSIDE THE BISON, THE STRANDED COPS CALLED FOR HELP...

I DON'T WANNA DIE, SARGE!! ≥SOB≤

PING PING

POLICE ICE

PULL YOURSELF TOGETHER ~ WE'RE NOT GONNA ≥GULP≤ DIE...

MORE BISONS ARRIVED TO RESCUE THE STRANDED TEAM. POLICE FIRED TENS OF THOUSANDS OF ROUNDS...

ON SEPT. 12, THE RCMP ASKED FOR THE ARMY'S 'ELITE' ANTI-TERRORIST UNIT JOINT TASK FORCE TWO (JTF2)...

IT'S LIKE A WAR-ZONE! OUR BOYS CAN'T TAKE IT!!

THAT SAME DAY, AN RCMP SNIPER FIRED ON A DEFENDER WALKING IN A NEGOTIATED NO-SHOOT ZONE...

POW!

ON SEPT. 13, LAKOTA SPIRITUAL LEADER ARVOL LOOKING HORSE WAS ALLOWED INTO THE CAMP...

ON SEPT. 16, ANOTHER LAKOTA SPIRITUAL LEADER~ JOHN STEVENS~ WAS PERMITTED ACCESS TO THE CAMP.

STEVENS ADVISED THEM THEIR WORK WAS DONE AND COULD NOW LEAVE...

ON SEPT. 17, THE DEFENDERS PLACED THEIR WEAPONS IN A FIRE AND WERE ARRESTED BY POLICE...

ALTOGETHER, THIS WAS THE RCMP'S LARGEST OPERATION IN CANADIAN HISTORY, INVOLVING OVER 450 COPS WITH 9 BISON APCS...

NATIVE YOUTH MOVEME...

THE TS'PETEN STANDOFF HAD A BIG IMPACT + INSPIRED A NEW GENERATION OF INDIGENOUS RESISTANCE IN 'BC'!

AAZHOODENA
IPPERWASH/STONEY POINT 1995

Dudley

DURING WORLD WAR II, CANADA TOOK THE STONEY POINT (AAZHOODENA) RESERVE FOR USE AS AN ARMY BASE. THE PEOPLE WERE RELOCATED TO A NEARBY REZ (KETTLE POINT).

Lake Huron / Ontario / Toronto / Sarnia / Aazhoodena / Lake Erie / 0 75 150 km

THE GOVERNMENT SAID IT WOULD RETURN THE LAND AFTER THE WAR, BUT IT NEVER DID...

IN 1993, 30 STONEY POINTERS MOVED IN AND OCCUPIED PART OF THE BASE. THEY STAYED FOR 2 YEARS...

SUMMER 1995: FRUSTRATED BY GOVERNMENT INACTION, THE PEOPLE STEPPED UP THEIR PROTESTS...

NOW HE'S TAKING A PISS!

THE ONTARIO PROVINCIAL POLICE (OPP) SET UP MORE SURVEILLANCE (POSING AS CAMPERS, A NEWS CREW, + AN AMBULANCE).

ON SEPT. 4, THE PEOPLE MOVED INTO IPPERWASH PROVINCIAL PARK - ALSO PART OF THEIR ORIGINAL RESERVE LANDS.

LET'S GET OUTTA HERE!

GOD DAMN INDIANS!

THAT NIGHT, CONFRONTATIONS WITH POLICE PATROLS OCCUR; ONE OPP CRUISER HAS A WINDOW SMASHED OUT...

EVEN THOUGH THE PEOPLE ARE UNARMED, THE OPP REQUEST MILITARY ASSISTANCE.

CRAZY COPS!

TO: CANADIAN ARMED FORCES FROM: ONTARIO PROVINCIAL POLICE RE: HELP!

THE OPP'S 'PROJECT MAPLE' WOULD INCLUDE 2 BISON APC S, HELICOPTERS, FLAK VESTS, GAS MASKS AND MORE...

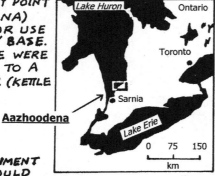

ON SEPT. 6, THE OPP SEALED OFF THE AREA WITH ROAD BLOCKS. MORE POLICE ARRIVED.

THAT SAME DAY THE PEOPLE FOUGHT WITH RIOT POLICE, WHO THREATENED DUDLEY GEORGE.

YOU'RE GONNA BE THE FIRST, DUDLEY!

WELCOME TO CANADA!

A BAND COUNCILOR FROM NEARBY KETTLE POINT TRIED TO INTERVENE BUT WAS ASSAULTED BY THE POLICE...

WAIT! THERE'S NO NEED FOR VIOL-ACK!

16-YEAR OLD NICHOLAS COTTRELLE THEN DROVE A BUS THRU' THE POLICE LINES TO STOP THE ASSAULT...

LOOK OUT!

VRROOMM

LATER THAT NIGHT, A RIOT SQUAD WITH 'LETHAL OVERWATCH' ENTERED THE PARK TO REMOVE THE PEOPLE...

THAT SPOTLIGHT IS BLINDING ME!

MEMBERS OF A TACTICAL RESPONSE UNIT (TRU) OPENED FIRE ON THE BUS, HITTING THE YOUTH AND KILLING A DOG.

POW POW

BAM BAM BAM

AT THIS TIME, SGT. KENNETH DEANE OF THE TRU FATALLY SHOT DUDLEY. ALMOST 2,000 ROUNDS WERE FIRED!

THE PEOPLE WERE VERY ANGRY WHEN THEY LEARNED THAT DUDLEY GEORGE HAD BEEN SHOT AND KILLED!

ON NEARBY HIGHWAY 21, THEY SET UP BURNING BLOCKADES AS EVEN MORE POLICE BEGAN ARRIVING (OVER 200).

THE POLICE CLAIMED THE PEOPLE HAD OPENED FIRE, BUT THIS WAS A LIE...

IT WAS SELF-DEFENSE!

THOUSANDS OF NATIVE PEOPLES ATTENDED DUDLEY'S FUNERAL ON SEPTEMBER 11/95.

THE GOVERNMENT ALSO ADMITTED THE LAND SHOULD HAVE BEEN RETURNED. TODAY, THE PEOPLE ONCE AGAIN LIVE IN STONEY POINT, WHERE DUDLEY GEORGE IS BURIED...

SERGEANT KENNETH DEANE WAS LATER CHARGED WITH CRIMINAL NEGLIGENCE CAUSING DEATH.

Remember Dudley George!

Dudley

Stoney Point • September 6, 1995

AAZHOODENA

IN 1997, HE WAS FOUND GUILTY. ALTHO' HE LIED DURING THE TRIAL, HE WAS GIVEN JUST 2 YEARS OF COMMUNITY SERVICE!

DURING THE '90s, INDIGENOUS MOVEMENTS IN SOUTH AMERICA ALSO BECAME STRONGER, ESPECIALLY IN ECUADOR, BOLIVIA, CHILE, & VENEZUELA...

MANY WERE UNITED IN FIGHTING NEO-LIBERAL **CAPITALIST** GLOBALIZATION.

IN CANADA, MORE NATIVE YOUTH BECAME INVOLVED IN **RESISTANCE.** IN 2000, THE MIQ'MAK OF BURNT CHURCH FOUGHT FOR FISHING RIGHTS AGAINST 100s OF POLICE...

IN 2006, THE SIX NATIONS LAND RECLAMATION WAS ATTACKED BY ONTARIO POLICE, SETTING OFF A MONTHS-LONG CONFRONTATION. ROADS, HIGHWAYS & TRAINS WERE BLOCKADED.

THIS IS THE **WORLD** WE LIVE IN, AND THE **HISTORY** THAT HAS MADE US WHO WE ARE. GENERATION AFTER GENERATION, OUR PEOPLE'S **RESISTANCE** AGAINST EUROPEAN COLONIZATION HAS CONTINUED.

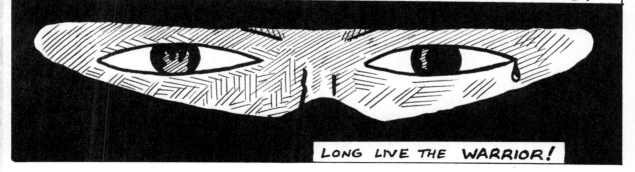

LONG LIVE THE **WARRIOR!**

GORD HILL is a member of the Kwakwaka'wakw nation whose territory is located on northern Vancouver Island and adjacent mainland in the province of "British Columbia." He is descended from Scottish and Tlingit great-grandparents. Since 1990, Gord has been involved in the Indigenous people's movement, including solidarity with the 1990 Oka Crisis, the 1992 500 Years of Resistance campaign, solidarity with the 1994 New Year's Zapatista Uprising, the 1995 Gustafsen Lake and Ipperwash standoffs, the Native Youth Movement (including the 1997-98 occupations of the BC Treaty Commission offices), the 1999 anti-WTO protests, the Cheam fisheries dispute (1999), the 2001 Summit of the Americas riots, the Skwelkwek'welt campaign (Sun Peaks, 2003–06), and most recently the anti-2010 Olympics campaign. He lives in Vancouver.

WARD CHURCHILL is a well-known activist and scholar of mixed-blood Cherokee descent. Currently a member of the elders council of the original Rainbow Coalition established in 1969 by Black Panther leader Fred Hampton in Chicago, he has been among the leadership of Colorado AIM for thirty years. Among his two dozen books are *A Little Matter of Genocide* (1997), *Pacifism as Pathology* (1998), and *Acts of Rebellion* (2003).